CALL AND RESPONSE

Jesuit Journeys in Faith

Call and Response

Jesuit Journeys in Faith

Edited by
Frances Makower RSCJ

Hodder & Stoughton
LONDON SYDNEY AUCKLAND

First published in Great Britain in 1994
by Hodder and Stoughton Ltd,
a division of Hodder Headline PLC

10 9 8 7 6 5 4 3 2 1

British Library Cataloguing in Publication Data

Call and Response: Jesuit Journeys in Faith
I. Makower, Frances
255.53

ISBN 0 340 60892 7

Typeset by Hewer Text Composition Services, Edinburgh
Printed and bound in Great Britain by
Cox & Wyman Ltd, Reading, Berkshire

Hodder and Stoughton Ltd,
A division of Hodder Headline PLC
338 Euston Road
London NW1 3BH

Contents

To Patrick, an unfailing
companion, friend and
guide on my journey.

Acknowledgements

I am most grateful to the Society of Jesus for their generous co-operation and assistance. In particular I want to thank Gerald O'Collins, for his initial and constant support; William Barry, John English, Michael Hurley, Nicholas King, Peter Knott, Patrick Purnell and Peter Steele for taking time from busy lives to produce valuable contributions; and Michael Ivens, David Lonsdale and Dermot Prescot for their critical advice. My thanks go also to Sister Eileen Whitehead, the secretary at the London provincialate.

To the charity Sequal I also owe much. As a result of a spinal disease, I had been unable to use a normal keyboard for some years. Sequal has provided a voice-activated computer which allows me to do with my voice all that I previously did with my hands. However, this marvel of technology would have been useless without the patient instruction of Hannah Grey. I am also most grateful for the grant I received from the Authors' Foundation.

My editor Carolyn Armitage has been unfailing in her encouragement and support; my community family and friends have patiently sustained me; and Teresa de Bertodano, who guided my first literary endeavours, has continued to be a sympathetic mentor and friend. All that I have received outweighs my slender resources, but since my coinage is prayer, I confidently entrust to the Lord all who have been involved in this project, together with all future readers.

Frances Makower
Roehampton 1994

The Training of a Jesuit

In the text of this book there are many references to the 'training' of a Jesuit. The following explanation may help readers to understand some of the terms used regarding the training process.

It should be noted that the 'training' has changed and developed over the years. Certain aspects of the training which the older writers in this collection would have received were different to that which the younger ones underwent. Further, 'training' differs from one part of the world to another. However, the following will elucidate the text for the reader.

Novitiate: On entering the Society, a man spends his first two years doing his novitiate. It is a period of time when he seeks to confirm his vocation to the Society and the Society considers whether or not he is a likely recruit. During the novitiate he will make the full 'Exercises', study the history of the Society, reflect upon its nature and engage in a variety of apostolic activities.

Juniorate: One or two years immediately following the novitiate, when a scholastic (see 'Grades' in Glossary) will round off his pre-university education. The juniorate no longer exists in some parts of the world, but has been maintained in others.

Regency: This is a period of one or two years in which the scholastic engages in some form of apostolic work; the kind of work can vary from teaching in a secondary school to giving retreats to helping refugees. Regency will usually take place just before the four years' study of theology (see below).

Studies – philosophy, theology and other areas: If the

scholastic does not have a degree on entering, he may do one in some 'secular' subject such as English or psychology. Every scholastic will spend two years studying philosophy and four years theology. Ordination to the priesthood follows theology.

Tertian year (tertianship): The tertianship is the final period of formation (see 'Tertian Year' in Glossary).

Final vows: A Jesuit will take his final vows some time after he has completed his tertianship (see 'Grades' in Glossary).

Gerald O'Collins SJ

Gerald O'Collins SJ was born in Melbourne, Australia in 1931. Until he was thirteen he was educated at home, apart from one year in primary school to which he rode on horseback. Between 1944 and 1948 he was a boarder at Xavier College in Melbourne which was run by the Jesuits. He joined the Society in 1950 and completed his studies at Melbourne University, Heythrop College, London (now a part of London University), and Cambridge University where in 1968 he received a doctorate in theology. Since 1974 he has taught full-time at the Gregorian University in Rome where he was Dean of Theology between 1985 and 1991. He is the author of twenty-eight books on various subjects including theology, spirituality and history, and he has lectured at colleges and universities in several countries including Ireland, the United Kingdom, the USA and Australia.

Introduction

Even before 1968 there was a goodly flow of books and articles by religious men and women who resolved their cases of conscience by 'leaping over the wall'. Such literature grew to a flood during the seventies and eighties.

We are all familiar with stories of those who, in their middle years, began listening to music from a different drummer. They felt constrained to leave the ministry and/or religious life, change deep allegiances and march off in a new direction. But must it always be a mark of integrity to resolve a fierce crisis by taking a fresh path in life? Could the claims of conscience also keep men and women striding along the same road, even if it often seems the road less travelled?

This book gathers the personal faith stories of eight contemporary Jesuits. They have worked at and developed their ideals in the nitty-gritty not only of flawed human institutions but also of their own growth as human beings who hunger to follow Jesus more closely. They have constantly faced the challenge of not letting their dreams fade and die. I found their stories a compelling read.

Some have obviously gone through agony on their pilgrimage. I was struck by the pain from within suffered by Patrick Purnell and the pain from without endured by Cecil McGarry. But we do not find anywhere in these eight stories a whiff of what Cecil calls 'the evil spirit of self-pity'. Dramatic incidents mark many of these faith journeys – from Nicholas King abruptly losing his father just as he began his Jesuit life to the turning-point for Peter Knott when he unexpectedly found himself ministering at an aircrash outside London. Over a hundred people had been killed and he blessed a tiny girl as she died.

The contributors to this book came from Australia, the United States, Canada, Ireland and the United Kingdom.

Two of them now work in Africa. What they have done and do as Jesuit priests also spreads them out very widely – as teachers, administrators and spiritual directors. One is a distinguished poet, another a psychologist and yet another a full-time ecumenist or minister for unity between the churches. One moved from chaplaincy work at Heathrow Airport to become chaplain at nearby Eton College.

The variety of ministries is stunning, but running through these eight stories is a common thirst to be with Jesus and to serve all his people. These ceaselessly busy men have had to learn over and over again how to cope with the tension between activity for others and prayer at the still centre of their lives.

The eight Jesuits have struggled with the enigma of divine love in a human world of terrifying violence, mass injustice and countless victims. They have learned, at times very painfully, not to allow disillusion to sap their strength as they cope with the ugly side of institutional Christianity. They have known the turmoil of putting into practice the Second Vatican Council's dream for the Church and the world. With hindsight they glimpse God writing straight with the crooked lines we trace in our church and our world.

Why have these eight sensitive and educated men soldiered on in the Society of Jesus? Some have experienced the deep, human pull of a life-giving relationship with a woman. None have escaped disturbing misunderstandings and failures in their ministry, and all knew how well they could succeed elsewhere should they walk out on their Jesuit commitment.

They have remained Jesuits basically because of a persistent feeling of being where they should be with Jesus. 'What else can I do?' (Purnell). 'What more could I ask?' (Barry). 'I *know* this is where I belong' (Knott). It is as Jesuits that they find their way to be themselves and travel home to God. It has been the only thing they could do with their lives if they wished to be true to themselves and to Jesus.

What has kept them going and growing? At times it was help from some other person who was there at the right time. Saintly Jesuit leaders like Pedro Arrupe, the late Superior General, and Paul Kennedy, a famed tertian master, exercised a profound impact on several of our authors. For some it was a case of stumbling across the right book at the right time. How I resonate with Nick King's example! For him it was a book by Carlo Carretto; for me it was Frances de Sales' *Introduction to a Devout Life*. Their families, fellow Jesuits and other friends have conspired to carry them along. As Michael Hurley puts it, being a Jesuit means enjoying a home all over the world. They speak of a voice calling from within, a sense of Jesus at their side or the energy of divine love at work in their world.

For many years I have known and been inspired by several of these eight authors. In reading all their contributions I have discovered again and more richly what I have always loved about Jesuits – the constantly high ideals that do not, however, lapse into fanaticism. Other readers from very different backgrounds will find in these stories the chance to deepen their own faith in God and to satisfy their spiritual hunger for Jesus.

The editor, Frances Makower, is more than just another part of this amazing packet. Years ago she injured her back at school, had radical and pioneering surgery which went badly wrong and necessitated both further operations and over twelve months in hospital in plaster beds and on skull traction – a ten-pound weight acting as a counter to body weight. But, as she told me, 'there were good moments and in one of these I slipped through the medicals and was accepted as a Religious of the Sacred Heart of Jesus. By then I was thirty-seven and had waited thirteen years. God only knows how I got through!'

Since 1971 Frances has worn a neck brace in addition to the surgical support prescribed after the original operation. 'All of this,' she agrees, 'creates an effective, do-it-yourself mortification kit.' In 1985, when she went to her present convent-home in Roehampton (London), she had to give up her work with homeless youngsters and drug abusers. She began writing. By that time arthritis was taking its toll and in 1989 her fingers could no longer cope with a keyboard. So writing had to go. But in 1992, Sequal, a charity which specialises in help with communications, lent her a voice-activated computer which put her back on the road of writing. In 1994, besides this book, two other books by Frances are to be published.

Chapter One of this book lets something of Frances shine through – something of her rich, courageous humanity. Her eight authors, as well as myself, are still very much on the road. With faith and love Frances has worked away in the room from which she can hardly stir, an urban hermit who follows and supports us pilgrims. If this book witnesses to the faith journeys and spiritual experience of eight Jesuits, it also witnesses to the spiritual greatness of Frances and what she has let divine love do to her and through her.

Gerald O'Collins SJ
The Gregorian University, Rome
13 October 1993

Frances Makower RSCJ

Born in London in 1930, Frances Makower was brought up as a liberal Jew. Educated at Roedean, a boarding school in south-east England, and Oxford University where she took a degree in Modern History, she taught for some years before working for Kaleidoscope, a London project for homeless youngsters and drug abusers. In 1952 she became a Roman Catholic and attempted to join the Society of the Sacred Heart, but failed the medical on account of a spinal injury incurred at school. Thirteen years later, during a period of remission, she passed the necessary medical. She has been a member of the Duchesne Sacred Heart Community since 1985. She has written several books, and although she now requires the assistance of a voice-activated computer, she is having three books published in 1994.

Chapter One

Jesuits – Who Are They?

In 1521 a cannon ball shattered a leg, changed a life and brought to birth a religious order whose radical influence is still with us. Ignatius of Loyola, a Basque from the north-west region of Spain, was wounded in a border skirmish as he tried to defend Pamplona against the French. He was about thirty at the time, a passionate young blood of such vanity that he chose the agony of prolonged surgery – no anaesthetic, of course – in preference to a deformed limb which could no longer sport the long high boot and close-fitting hose dictated by fashion.

As the seventh and youngest son of an impoverished nobleman, Ignatius' choice of career had been limited to the church or the army – he received some preparation for both. As a child he was taught to read and write and was even tonsured; as an adolescent he was sent to join the household of the King's treasurer to learn the courtly arts. There he was in his element, when not active in following the chase, bearing arms or flirting with women, he was engrossed in romantic novels, feeding his extravagant day-dreams.

Thus, when he had been brought home and was beginning to recover from the 'butchery' (his own term) required for the resetting of his shattered leg, his first request was for something to read. There were only two books in the castle of Loyola: A Life of Christ, and a History of the Saints. Boredom drove him to glance through their pages. He became increasingly captivated and gradually, over the months his absorption in Jesus, Mary his mother and the exploits of the saints began to rival and finally replace his worldly day-dreams. In this first spiritual awakening, Ignatius displayed a rare ability to reflect on his own inner reactions.

He found that while his day-dreams about the saints left him at peace and full of joy, his romantic reveries left him empty, dry and restless. This was the first step of discernment, or the testing of spirits, which was to have a major role in his spirituality. He started to keep a spiritual notebook using red ink for notes on Jesus, and blue for Mary.

Ignatius had fallen in love and transferred his loyalty and devotion to God, hook, line and sinker! He left the family castle to travel to the Holy Land by way of the Benedictine abbey of Montserrat in north-eastern Spain. There he made an all-night vigil before the famous 'black madonna' and exchanged his clothes with a beggar. He then stopped off at the small nearby town of Manresa in order to note down a few reflections. The 'stop' lasted ten months. He said of that period that God treated him just as a school-master treats a small boy. Ignatius neglected his appearance, begged for his food and undertook such ferocious penance that he brought himself to the brink of death. After a period of initial joy, he entered into a profound spiritual crisis, followed by a flood of spiritual understanding. Throughout his life he frequently experienced mystical graces. During this time his main work was the discovery of a way to find God in all things. He began to learn that true happiness can only be found in doing the will of God and becoming a co-worker for the Kingdom. This experience, duly noted in his book, was to become 'The Spiritual Exercises' which embody Ignatius' spirituality and have brought succeeding generations to the service of the Kingdom.

Finally, passionate to walk in the earthly steps of his saviour, he left Manresa in 1523 on the first leg of his pilgrimage to Jerusalem. He yearned to spread the good news among the Turks, the current rulers of the Holy Land, but relations between the Christian guardians of the holy places and their Turkish rulers were too fragile to be exposed to the enthusiasm of a convert fanatic; he was forbidden to stay and after nineteen ecstatic days he was back on board for the hazardous three-month return voyage to Europe. Undaunted, he accepted that he had been mistaken in his discernment of God's will and returned to Spain.

Ignatius was afire with the love of God and consumed by the need to spread that fire to all who would listen. Many would, but his was the Spain of the Holy Inquisition which had efficient and unspeakably brutal ways of protecting the faith. Ignatius' only hope of preaching was as a priest – which at the least meant Latin, of which he had none. He was already thirty-three, but undeterred, he joined a class of schoolboys. Ignatius was never a person to be interested in the less – indeed, for God he always wanted more, but he was not a natural scholar and long years of study lay ahead.

During these years he was no more able to desist from talking of God than from drawing breath. This inevitably brought trouble and in 1527 he spent several weeks in chains in the jail of Salamanca. Even when his preaching had finally been proved blameless and he was freed, hampering restrictions were placed on his ability to help others. This was an impossible situation, so he shook the dust of Spain from his feet and made for Paris, where in 1528 he began his studies afresh.

Six years later he had so fired fellow students that six of them joined him at the church at Montmartre where Peter Faber, the one priest among them, said Mass and they all made vows of poverty, chastity and pilgrimage to Jerusalem.[1] Should this last prove impossible – access to Turkish-controlled Holy Land was anything but assured at this time – they agreed to put themselves under the direct authority of the Pope.

Why the Pope? Sixteenth-century Europe was expanding. To the west, Columbus had 'discovered' America in 1492 (one year after Ignatius' birth), to the east, the Portuguese were penetrating further into Africa and the South Atlantic and extending exploration to the East Indies and beyond. All these 'new' lands, teeming with souls awaiting salvation, drew these fiery young men as air draws flame. They believed that they would win greater glory for God and be enabled to do more for souls if they put themselves at the immediate disposal of the Pope. Having completed their studies they gathered in Venice where they hoped to embark for Jerusalem. As they waited they worked in the hospitals. There, in 1537, Ignatius and the five others were ordained.

Their vows taken at Montmartre were a step towards the foundation of a new religious order, although they had little idea of this at the time. All were radically committed to the 'helping of souls', and hence to apostolic work. The companions, now expanded to ten, had gathered in Rome where the winter of 1538–9 was particularly severe, so by day they devoted themselves to the sick and the poor, while at night in prayer and discernment they drew up the basic rules for 'The Society of Jesus', the name which they had unanimously chosen for their new religious order. They were agreed that no activity was to take priority over their work of saving souls; even previously accepted methods of prayer and customs of religious life must give way to the needs of the apostolate. Divine Office therefore would be said in private rather than sung in choir, and liturgies kept simple. As students under Ignatius' inspiration, they had each experienced 'finding God in all things' – they would serve God by serving others as contemplatives in action. Where they lived, in or out of community, would be dependent upon the demands of the apostolate; their dress would conform to that of simple clerics but their vows of chastity, poverty and obedience would be absolute.

Such a novel interpretation of religious life was unlikely to find favour in Rome where the climate was hostile to religious communities whose numbers were declining and whose practice was held to have become lax. Yet within a year, the numerous recommendations secured by Ignatius, combined with constant, determined prayer had melted all opposition. In September 1540 Pope Paul III officially approved the Society of Jesus and in the following year Ignatius himself was unanimously elected Superior General. This post, accepted with great reluctance, tied him to a desk in Rome where he spent his remaining years guiding his new and radical Society and working on its Constitutions. The Society continued to expand and when Ignatius died in 1556 the members of the Society of Jesus numbered over one thousand.

From the earliest days the young Jesuit priests were much in demand, hence Francis Xavier left Rome on the first leg of his journey east in March 1540, six months ahead of official recognition. When he died twelve years later he had laid the groundwork for a flourishing future mission based in India and extending to the East Indies, Japan and even China.

He also left basic instructions in the faith in Tamil, Malayan and Japanese, an administration centred in Goa to support and train future Jesuit missioners, and hundreds of letters of inspiration and exhortation sent both to Jesuits and lay people in Europe and the East.

Xavier's letters, many of which have survived, contain clues to his success together with the cost to himself. His isolation can be gauged by the 300-mile winter trek that he once undertook in order to hand his letters in person to a certain captain who was returning from Japan to Europe. All the records depict an impatient, affectionate enthusiast who, they said, had laughter in his mouth. He was tirelessly devoted to God and every man, woman or child lucky enough to cross his path – the greater their need, the deeper was his compassion. He travelled hundreds of thousands of miles, generally in appalling conditions, and wherever he went he gave away his food, his clothes, his bed. He nursed lepers, worked among prisoners in stinking jails and walked hundreds of miles desperately trying to communicate the love of God to primitive pearl fishermen or cultivated Japanese Buddhists or even so-called Christian merchants.

Some believe that Xavier was a gifted linguist; he was not. 'May it please God our Lord,' he implored, 'give us language.' We have his own graphic description of assimilating Tamil. Finding one of the pearl fishermen with a smattering of Portuguese, he got him to translate the basic prayers, these he wrote down in some fashion and then laboriously learnt by rote. He used the same lengthy process to instruct Malay hunters and Japanese land-owners. Xavier's talent was for souls rather than tongues, but his love was unbounded and he was himself deeply loved. His was the love that led to the spreading of the Christian faith to tens, hundreds and thousands of souls in India, the East Indies and the Far East. His was indeed an outstanding example of heroic missionary work and yet what he was doing was typical of the work of many Jesuits.

In the early years of the Society the majority of missioners came from Spain and Portugal – countries in the van of colonisation. By the seventeenth century the French had joined the colonial club and were trading down the Great Lakes of Canada with the native Indians. In 1632 French

Jesuits followed the traders and established a station near Quebec. They had some success in sharing the good news with the Algonguin, but the Hurons were a primitive people who moved with the herds down the St Lawrence river and along the shores of the Great Lakes. Anyone attempting to bring the good news to the Hurons must be prepared to share their simple life.

For sixteen years (1633–49) Jean de Brébeuf did precisely that. Throughout the daylight hours he paddled their canoes, stopping only to porter the boats and heavy goods around the numerous waterfalls. At night he and his fellow Jesuits slept in primitive wood cabins, ate sagamite (an Indian-type porridge which he compared to wallpaper paste), and lacked even a light by which to read a breviary. They cheerfully supported these hardships in the belief that they would thus gain the respect of the Indians; they were not mistaken. Through the work of these early missionaries, the Huron Christian Community was established in the Ontario area and the continuous history of the native Canadian Church can be traced back to this time. The Jesuits, however, became caught in the political turmoil between the English and French, and the Iroquois and the Hurons. In 1649 Brébeuf was brutally martyred by renegade Iroquois and shortly after three more Jesuits suffered the same fate. The Hurons became dispersed and the Canadian mission, established with such self-sacrifice and hardship, had to be abandoned. All was far from lost, however, for in Canada the Hurons persevered in their faith and in France the news of the heroic martyrs created enthusiasm for the missions. Men poured into the noviceships and ten years later the Canadian mission was reopened.

In South America the Jesuit missionaries formed an international group which achieved 'the Paraguay Reductions' – a remarkable experiment in social engineering that thrived throughout the seventeenth century and for the first half of the eighteenth.

Moving constantly west to escape the slavers, who looked on Indians as 'walking gold', they established fifty-seven self-supporting Christian villages populated by over a hundred thousand Indians. The reductions were scattered over a region about the size of Texas. Each village, centred around a plaza, was dominated by the church where the inhabitants celebrated liturgies with their own music and song. Every family owned a home and had a plot to till outside the village; food was rationed and therefore plentiful. Jesuits skilled in carpentry, agriculture, metal work, architecture and printing trained the Indians and trade flourished between the different villages in the Reductions.

This remarkable experiment came to an end because of the greed of the Spanish and Portuguese merchants who were ruthlessly determined to lay hands on the mythical wealth, rumoured to be amassed in the Reductions. By the terms of a treaty between Spain and Portugal, frontier borders were redrawn in 1750. Thirty thousand Christian Indians and missionaries were ordered to abandon their homes and villages from seven Reductions. The fragile trust between the Jesuits and Indians was broken; the Indians rebelled and were inevitably defeated. A generation later, King Charles of Spain expelled all Jesuits from his colonies for reasons that he refused to divulge.

Some Jesuits lived ordinary, not to say hum-drum lives. From the beginning – like any other group – they were dogged by personality clashes, self-seeking and politicking, but the fact remains that these various enterprises portray men of outstanding courage and 'by their fruits you will know them'. What was their secret? The answer, in part, lies in the mystery of God's grace, but much can be learnt from Ignatius – from his life, his aims and methods. When, in 1541, he had been unanimously elected Superior General, he had needed some persuasion that God was indeed calling him to this responsibility. Once convinced, however, he undertook the unwanted office with customary zeal, tempered by wisdom and compassion learnt from his own mistakes. The Constitutions, the rapidly developing shape of the apostolate both within Europe and beyond, and the formation of Jesuit recruits all carry the stamp of his inspiration.

Ignatius was neither the first nor the last to introduce religious reform, but his capacity to reflect on his own spiritual experience, to note it down and cull from it methods that could be passed on – most notably 'The Spiritual Exercises' – was unusual, not to say unique. He was writing about his own conversion and the way in which he had come to find God in all things. Furthermore, while his directions are clear, direct and detailed they have an inbuilt flexibility which has enabled succeeding generations of men and women, both lay and religious, to use the 'Exercises', either in full or in an abbreviated form.

Guided by his own experience, Ignatius started from the premise that while true happiness, that is to say the fulfilment that God intends, is to be found only in doing God's will, selfishness and sin militate against such dependence on God. Thus for those who have the desire, or at least desire the desire to become true followers of Christ and co-workers of the Kingdom, he drew up a series of meditations and contemplations, based principally upon the Gospels. Under the guidance of a competent 'director' and over a period of four weeks, a 'retreatant' is led through a process of prayer, reflection and discernment to a deeper knowledge of the mind and heart of Christ. The retreatant is offered a framework for guidance in daily life and encouraged to find God in all things – the fundamental of Ignatian spirituality. Lest this seem too easy, it must be said that the 'Exercises' are neither a soft option nor a passport to instant, press-button holiness. No one understood better than Ignatius that the 'Exercises', at least in full, were not for everyone. In those early days in Paris he waited several years before directing Francis Xavier – and he described Francis as 'the hardest nut he ever had to crack'. For Jesuits, however, the 'Exercises' are an essential part of formation and are undertaken in their full length at least twice – at the beginning and end of their training.

The extent and thoroughness of formation in the Society of Jesus is indicated by its length – at least a decade and often longer. Peter-Hans Kolvenbach, elected Superior General in 1983, said of Ignatius that he aimed at the mobilisation of the entire human potential. Thus in addition to theology – obligatory for all Jesuit priests – Ignatius typically insisted on the study of languages, literature and philosophy. In the words of George Ganss SJ, the editor of the English edition of the Constitutions, 'he aimed to form [his men] into cultivated persons who would be able and eager to take a capable part in the social, cultural and religious life of their era and leaven their environment with the principles of Christ'. Thus, in the early years, Ignatius' most pressing task was to make provision for this all-round education. He acted with typical speed. Within the first four years of the Society's life he had established seven residences for his young 'scholastics', placing them within easy reach of universities. Jesuit teachers were soon drafted into the residences which became regular schools and colleges. Almost immediately a clamour arose demanding the admission of lay students. This was agreed and when Ignatius died, thirty-three schools already existed in Europe and a further six were in the pipeline.

Thus, while Jesuits were becoming the missionaries of 'the new worlds' of the seventeenth and eighteenth centuries, they were also becoming the teachers of Europe. Their schools were 'networked', to use a contemporary term, and their studies and administration carefully monitored. In 1599, after nearly fifty years of trial and critique, the *Ratio Studiorum* or Plan of Studies was published which was to govern procedure and curricula in all Jesuit schools for the best part of two centuries. The Plan also had an indelible influence on virtually all educational practice in Europe and beyond.

By their fruits you will know them and the fruit had barely time to ripen before it was in general demand. The consequent growth and expansion of the Society was phenomenal. When Ignatius died in 1556, less than sixteen years after the official recognition of the Society, its members already numbered over a thousand and had spread around Europe, Africa, South America, the West Indies, India and many areas of the Far East.

From the earliest days Ignatius understood the key role of communication both as a means of furthering the apostolate and sustaining unity. Those in authority were bound under obedience to write to him regularly with detailed news and it is clear that he was rigorous in his expectations of his correspondents, both in terms of style and content. Nearly seven thousand letters written, dictated or approved by Ignatius himself have survived. They were frequently copied and sent on to friends or well-wishers as well as to 'ours' (Jesuits), and Ignatius relied on the letters for that union of hearts which is the *sine qua non* of the Society. While many are addressed to his own men, Ignatius kept up an amazingly

large correspondence with friends and acquaintances outside
– churchmen and lay people, well-wishers and detractors and
also a number of women.

To later generations the letters offer glimpses of a brilliant
administrator at work, a compassionate friend who makes
time to write letters of condolence: 'God knows that I have
kept you and do still keep you very close to my heart.' He
scolds, encourages and commiserates with his men: 'It is not
surprising that this occupation [theology] usually brings on a
certain dryness.' He is concerned for their health, and writes
to one: 'Be persuaded that you are acting under obedience in
whatever you do to recreate yourself in the Lord as a means
to recover your health.' Perhaps the most telling letter is
that to Father Barreto, written in 1553 at the time when
unconfirmed rumours of the death of Francis Xavier were
reaching Europe. Even at this moment of sorrowful anxiety,
Ignatius acted with characteristic wisdom: 'If Francis is dead,'
he wrote to Father Barreto, 'I confirm you in the office of
provincial. If he is still alive, then the decision must be made
by him.' Ignatius' trust in those to whom he had given
authority is a hallmark of his government. His instructions
are clear, but again and again he adds the phrase, 'if it can
be done.'

Ignatius was admirably served by his secretary, Juan de
Polanco SJ, but for all that the sheer volume of work
he accomplished was astounding. He actively governed
the far-flung and expanding Society, while at the same
time writing the Constitutions of this first truly apostolic
order which was constantly breaking new ground. Like
the letters, the Constitutions clearly mirror the person of
Ignatius; the phrase 'as discreet charity allows', constantly
recurs underlining the humanity of a man who advocated
the playing of music as a means of relief to the sick.

Ignatius demanded and received total obedience, indeed
'Jesuit obedience' adopted by so many religious communities
is famous – not to say infamous. A superior might, for
example, come to believe that for the greater glory of God
one of his men should undertake a different mission. The
man in question might disagree in which case he had both
the right and the duty to counter the proposed change in the
strongest possible terms. The superior is duty bound both to

listen and to give due weight to every counter argument, but as and when he sees fit the superior makes the decision and his man obeys. The obedience demanded of Jesuits is indeed absolute, but it should not be confused with that imposed by a totalitarian dictator. Clause 284 of the Constitutions states that obedience can never override the 'clear judgement of conscience'.

Such a regime exercised in a hierarchical organisation is obviously open to abuse and the risk of exploitation. In a few cases injustice has caused suffering, but in general the Jesuit system of obedience has been a reliable tool in the work for souls, largely because it is based on trust. At regular intervals each man is required to give an account of his conscience to his superior – or in the words of a modern document, 'The religious . . . should try to make himself known, with his gifts and limitations, his desires, difficulties and ideas, through a confiding, familiar and candid colloquy, about which the superior is held to absolute secrecy' (GC 31 275). This observance is unique to the Jesuit order and enables a superior to know his men and, provided authority is exercised with the wisdom and discreet charity laid down by the Constitutions, superiors should be in a position to govern for the greater glory of God, service to all people and the happiness of the members of the Society. With some exceptions, this generally has been the case both in the lifetime of Ignatius and subsequently.

Ignatius died in 1556, and the simplicity of his death was in marked contrast to the drama of his first steps in the spiritual life. Knowing that he was going to die, he asked Polanco to obtain a blessing for him from the Pope (Paul IV). Neither Polanco nor the physician believed that death was imminent; Polanco continued with his letters and Ignatius did not wait for the blessing. He died early in the morning of 31 July, leaving the Society with sound foundations for a successful future.

Success, however, never comes cheap, and by the middle of the eighteenth century the Jesuits were thoroughly feared and mistrusted. In 1773 the storm broke. The Bourbons demanded the Society's head on a platter, threatening that should Pope Gregory XIV refuse to comply with their demand for the suppression of the Society, they would follow the precedent established by Henry VIII of England and set up their own national churches, independent of Rome. Gregory was frail, sick and under immense pressure. The Bourbons controlled Spain, Portugal, Austria and Naples. With this very real threat of schism, the outcome was inevitable. In 1773 the Pope cashed the Jesuits' fourth vow of obedience to the papacy and issued a Bull suppressing the Society, thereby inviting its members to commit what might be termed spiritual hara-kiri.

The Society's properties were confiscated and more than 23,000 Jesuits left destitute; many were exiled and almost all responded with heroism. Several, including Lorenzo Ricci, the general, were thrown in prison and died there. More than 600 colleges, 150 seminaries and twenty universities were closed in Europe within the space of ten years. Catherine the Great of Russia was the only ruler who had sufficient regard for her subjects to resist the papacy, so the suppression was never total. For a time the Jesuits in Russia were caught between Catherine's refusal to countenance the Bull of suppression and their own vowed obedience to the Pope, but Catherine's determination won the day and a papal exception was granted for the Society to exist in Russia.

Within a generation, however, the storm of opposition was on the wane; many church leaders who had previously allied themselves to the politicians began to understand that the attack on the Society was the prelude to the rationalists' attack on the church. It was said that one of the cardinals had remarked that 'the church lives very badly without the Jesuits'. Many agreed. In Russia, the historian William Bangert SJ records, 'They began to put together, piece by piece, the body of the former Society.' By 1814, when Pope Pius VII, himself newly returned to the Vatican from captivity in France, issued the Bull reinstating the order, the superiors of Russia had already been accepted as Superior Generals of the Society.

Resurrection was rapid. In 1814 over seventy novices entered while 700 former Jesuits rejoined. By the end of the nineteenth century the Society had once again become a force in the church with about 15,000 members and expansion under way in North America and elsewhere, but sporadic national expulsions continued. At different times

Jesuits were expelled from France, Mexico, Portugal, Spain, Germany and from various Communist regimes.

In 1965 Pedro Arrupe was elected Superior General at the thirty-first General Congregation, the first Basque to be elected since Ignatius. The Congregation met with the specific intention of renewing the Society in accordance with the teaching of Vatican II. A decade later the thirty-second General Congregation was summoned to take stock of the Society in the light of ten years of change. At this congregation, in response to requests from Jesuits throughout the world, a decree was passed which has become the guiding principle of the apostolate:

What does it mean to be a companion of Jesus today? It means to engage in the spiritual combat proper to our time under the standard of the cross. The crucial struggle today is being waged on the field of faith and of the justice integral to it (GC 32 22).

and:

The road which leads to faith is identical with that which leads to justice. It is one which the pilgrim Church finds hard and laborious. In the gospel, faith and justice are inseparably linked, because 'faith works through love'. Faith and justice therefore must remain one: in our intention, in our actions, in the whole of our lives. (GC 32 28).

In 1993 there were approximately 24,000 Jesuits working in 113 countries. About 8,000 of these were involved in the teaching apostolate; between them they were educating about one and a half million students. Peter-Hans Kolvenbach, elected General in 1983, stated that the apostolate of education will maintain its primary place in the apostolate. The Society of Jesus remains one of the largest missionary congregations in the church and is operating in most of the developing world.

Jesuits work increasingly with lay people, for there is a thrust towards empowering them, and they are now to be found giving the 'Exercises', leading retreats, running parishes and organising schools. Members of the Society are working in refugee camps, with the media, with ecumenical or multi-faith projects, at centres for concern and centres of faith and justice. They continue to give the 'Spiritual Exercises', direct retreats, run prayer workshops, do pastoral work and serve the church as bishops and cardinals. According to the constitutions, no Jesuit may become a bishop or cardinal without the express order of the Pope – in 1993, ninety-three Jesuits had been so ordered to serve as bishops and a further six as cardinals.

Pedro Arrupe, the former General, warned that there would be a price to pay in working for justice; no fewer than thirty-two men have given their lives since 1975 in the struggle to obtain human rights for oppressed peoples. The six Jesuits murdered, with their housekeeper and her daughter, in November 1989 at the University of Central America in San Salvador are probably the best known.

But a price has also been paid by the whole Society for their stand on human rights. In 1981 Pedro Arrupe suffered a serious stroke. The Constitutions made provision for such a contingency: a vicar general was to be appointed until an election for a new general took place. The Pope, himself the guardian of the Constitutions, appeared to ignore this provision and named the elderly Paolo Dezza SJ as his delegate with full powers over the Society. During the 1970s and early 1980s communication between the papacy and the Society generalate was at an all-time low. The Pope had been alarmed by the active participation of many Jesuits in the movement of liberal theology. If there was some support and sympathy for the Pope's action, there was also much indignation and anger. It was felt in some quarters that there had been an abuse of power.

In the event it is generally agreed that Paolo Dezza did an excellent job; he managed to carry the Society with him while regaining the confidence of John Paul II. With papal approval he summoned the thirty-third General Congregation and Peter-Hans Kolvenbach, the second Dutchman to hold the office of Superior General, was elected.

Jesuits continually ask, 'What does it mean to be a Christian?' and spend their lives attempting to live out the answer. There is an urgency to this question springing from the intense desire to 'help souls' – that same urgency that dominated Ignatius' life from the first moment of his conversion.

The desire to help others often leads to the desire to be part of a group. Many different groups have adopted Ignatian spirituality and have joined forces to create movements such as Christian Life Communities or Jesuit Volunteer Communities. In an age in which individuals tend to be identified by what they buy or what they own, people who are prepared to be identified by what they have received and acknowledge their dependence, buck the trend. They 'do justice'; they are key-workers for the Kingdom.

Ignatius drew up clear and demanding guide lines. From across the continents his vision has been understood by men who have themselves become members of the Society of Jesus. The subsequent chapters of this book portray eight such men – all contemporary Jesuits – whose lives give eloquent testimony to Ignatius and his vision.

Endnotes

1 From the early Middle Ages a pilgrimage to Jerusalem was reckoned to be the hardest and holiest act a Christian could perform on account of the hardships and dangers of both the journey and the hostility of the Turkish rulers to Christians.

Frances Makower RSCJ
London, UK

Nicholas King SJ

Nicholas King SJ was born in 1947 in Bath and educated at Stonyhurst, the Jesuit boarding school in the north of England and Oxford. In 1970 he joined the Jesuits and was ordained in 1980. Both before and after completing his training in the Society, he taught in a variety of institutions, both secondary and tertiary. In 1989 he went to teach Biblical Studies at St Joseph's Theological College, Natal, and is currently Dean of Studies there.

Chapter Two

Yes to the Future

In 1947 I was born into a staunchly Catholic family and into an awareness of a world that was divided into Catholics and non-Catholics. It was a matter of pride that not a drop of non-Catholic blood ran in our veins, and that Catholic martyrs adorned both sides of the family tree. It was not that we thought that non-Catholics were condemned to hell, nor did we avoid 'them'. It was simply that they were different. They did not go to Mass on Sundays and they did not eat fish on Fridays. This may seem odd but that is the way I saw the world upwards of forty years ago, at a time when the Second Vatican Council with its gale of fresh air was still some twenty years distant.

Since time began my family had been solicitors in the city of Bath, with a strong tradition of unselfish public service. Equally part of the family tradition was the sending of male children to Stonyhurst, a Jesuit boarding school in the north of England. This peculiarly English habit of parting with children for the greater part of the year should not be mistaken for lack of affection. My mother is still alive and I have a sister and two brothers; we love each other deeply, but we are not demonstrative and would be rather embarrassed to speak of our affection.

I was the eldest son and was duly sent to a Catholic preparatory school at the age of seven. This involved the painful and mysterious business of leaving home. On reflection, seven seems terribly young and I now regret it. I think I regretted it then, without being able to admit it, because in the course of my first term at the school I started to wet the bed, a humiliating ailment that lasted without much interruption for a further sixteen years until finally, as though

a tap had been turned off, it stopped when I entered the
Society of Jesus: a liberation that was, to me, little short of
miraculous.

The preparatory school was Catholic, and twice a week
priests came to say Mass, hear confessions and give Benediction.
Prayer was as much part of the scene as Latin irregular
verbs and the headmaster's terrifying gymshoe. At about this
time the thought of becoming a priest crossed my mind. I
have a suspicion that I rather admired a very dashing curate
in our home parish, and I can certainly recall being impressed
by the Pope's white robes, possibly through a confusion with
cricket, a sport for which I already had a passionate and
enduring affection.

I came to know priests at close quarters for the first
time when, at the age of thirteen, I went, as decreed,
to Stonyhurst. The notion of a vocation to the priesthood
immediately disappeared and did not resurface until the
end of my school days. Perhaps I did not like the priests
I saw; undeniably the Jesuits who ran Stonyhurst imposed
strict discipline and in the early days I can recall a degree
of fear. I know that I was fifteen years old before I stopped
locking myself in the lavatory on the train leaving Bath so
that I could have a good howl in private.

For most of my time at Stonyhurst I had not the smallest
thought of becoming a priest, although in hindsight I realise
that some essential groundwork was going on. I was, moreover,
aware that the Jesuits who taught us were rather an
impressive body of men, some of whom have subsequently
become well known. A small number of them instilled both
fear and dislike, but I now see that almost all gave themselves
unselfishly to our tedious adolescent eccentricities. They did
not teach us anything formally about the Society and its
history, but we soaked up a fair amount of the Jesuit
way of life.

Prayer was also important at that time. In our family it
was always taken for granted that we prayed morning and
evening, and that we visited the Catholic church in any town
that we passed through. Prayer was part of the background.
For all that, I look back in some astonishment at my
adolescent self, for I spent quite a long time in prayer after
daily Mass and at Holy Hour which I cheerfully attended

of my own volition. I also remember praying fiercely for an end to the wretched bed-wetting and my anger that my prayer went unheard. (When finally it did stop, it was years before I noticed the fact sufficiently to thank God for this deliverance.) In retrospect I am certain that to pray was an invitation from God, to which I was genuinely responding, however immaturely.

Towards the end of my time at Stonyhurst the thought of priesthood briefly resurfaced, this time presenting itself as a specific call to the Jesuits. I had not thought deeply about the difference between Jesuits and secular priests, but Jesuits were the priests I knew well. However, I rigorously suppressed the idea because by then I had calculated, correctly as it turned out, that I was likely to win a scholarship to Oxford. From this distance it seems providential that I did not take the idea of the priesthood seriously at that time, for I was hardly mature when I entered the noviceship at the age of twenty-three; it would have been catastrophic had I entered at eighteen.

So I gave a loud 'No' to all thought of the priesthood and at that time was attracted to a variety of schemes. I would become a barrister and a Conservative politician, or alternatively marry my current girlfriend, have thirteen children and support them all by becoming a social worker. I do not suppose that I had any real understanding of social work, but I believe I was becoming aware that society was not all it should be. In the meantime prayer had, I seem to remember, dropped away; certainly it had become drier.

Thus in October 1966, having gained a scholarship in Classics to St John's College, Oxford, where Edmund Campion, the Jesuit martyr of the sixteenth century had once been a tutor, I had a strong sense that the world was my personal oyster. But within a few short months there I was, asking to be admitted to the Society of Jesus.

In the event this decision came totally unexpected. I had arrived home from Oxford for my first vacation in December 1966 and on Christmas Eve went to church where I was on my knees waiting for our parish midnight Mass. Far from being 'lost in prayer', I recall a longing for a smoke; certainly I had not the smallest intention of pondering my future, but then I became aware that the only thing to do with my life, if I was to be happy, was to become a Jesuit. There was no weighing of pros and cons, simply a certainty and a clarity that has never left me. I told my family immediately and applied to the Society of Jesus, who had the good sense to tell me to finish my degree first.

So I knew where I was headed and given this certainty, the following years were surprisingly confused. On the one hand, I was decidedly a practising Catholic – this, despite occasional efforts to break out, was simply something I had to be. Almost every day I went to Mass, because to my surprise, I found it helped to bring the day together. This annoyed me slightly, for I had disliked the compulsory daily school Mass. On the other hand, this was also a time of fairly profound darkness when the existence of God quite often seemed very problematic and the church a good deal more so. At the time – the late sixties – all kinds of questioning was in the air, and the church, as ever, was an obvious target for healthy debate. Moreover, part of the benefit of a place like Oxford was the frequent encounter with intelligent and good people who thought that belief in God, Christianity and above all Catholicism was incoherent or even immoral.

As I look back I am aware of two other influences that made their mark at that time. The Oxford Dominican priory was opposite my college; I went to Mass there and met some of the Dominican students and priests. This was an eye-opener. Their tone was radical revolution rather than reform, and I discovered an unfamiliar and attractive side of Catholicism. I owe those men, including those who are now no longer Dominicans, a very great deal, and have admired the order ever since. Also I had by this time formed the habit of going to Lourdes each year. In the times when things seemed most obscure, when the defects of the institutional church seemed most repellent, and the existence of God most unlikely, I could not deny that there was something at Lourdes. At the Grotto there, late at night, there was an atmosphere of prayer that I could not resist; moreover, in working with sick people I discovered that I received far more than I gave.

Four years at university rushed by – a wonderful interlude. I was fairly idle, doing just enough study to get by without embarrassment. I was sociable, enjoying all kinds of parties and much sport. I cannot say that I regret much from these years, except perhaps the wasted intellectual opportunities, but I am also aware of considerable intellectual growth. Even a casual brush with philosophy is liable to sharpen one's claws for intellectual debate, and philosophy also had a marked effect on my faith. Oxford has always been a place where religion is talked about, and even though I was in something of an inner darkness for much of the time, I relished talking about it all. And finally it was at Oxford that I gained a lasting admiration for the Anglican tradition.

These, then, were years of growth. If for much of the time I experienced pain and darkness in my inner life, on another level I had a wonderful time enjoying the good life to the full. The certainty about becoming a Jesuit never left me, and so in 1970 I formally applied to become a novice; rather to my relief I was accepted. I can still recall the envy of some of my Oxford contemporaries – I knew where I was headed but they were still casting around.

The first week in the novitiate at Rainhill was traumatic. I entered on Monday 14 September which in the Catholic Church is venerated, aptly enough, as the feast of the Holy Cross. On Thursday 17 September my father had a massive heart-attack while running for a train, and on Saturday 19 September he died. So though I had not realised it at the time, I had said goodbye to him at Bristol Station that Monday morning. We shook hands, I recall, for nothing more intimate was our style, and I noticed that he had tears in his eyes, but callow young man that I was then, I was far too preoccupied with myself to respond sensitively. I have regretted ever since that we did not say a proper farewell. I am irked by the young man I then was, and have often wondered whether my father had some premonition that we should not see each other again.

So in less than a week I was home again, not because, as I had feared, I had been turned away, but to attend my father's funeral. That this was a painful time hardly needs saying, and returning to the noviceship two days after the funeral was one of the hardest things I have ever done; but alongside our grief we experienced, quite remarkably, a sense of resurrection peace and joy. This went deeper than the pain and made my return to the noviceship possible.

The return was not a good experience. I needed to talk, but the novice-master, a man whom I already knew I could talk to, was away for the weekend. I remember my misery as I worked in the garden that Saturday and wondered what in heaven's name I was doing.

The two years of novitiate were, on the whole, difficult. I can still recall the sense of bliss as I boarded a train for London on the first leg of a journey to Lourdes where, to my surprise, I was being sent on a brief pilgrimage. I bought a packet of cigarettes with the 'pocket money' I had been given and the sense of luxury as I inhaled and contemplated the next few days of freedom is with me still. However, I gained a great deal from the experience of the noviceship where I read widely on the history of the Society and its Constitutions. I also received formation in prayer, which created a lifetime's habit for which I am profoundly grateful. The experience of 'The Spiritual Exercises', while exceedingly dark in places, was nevertheless life-transforming. So, too, in a different way were the various pastoral experiments which sent us off to the Liverpool docks and factories to work with all manner of people, including immigrants. For three months I stayed in Dublin at the novitiate of the Irish province and was there on 'Bloody Sunday' when British troops shot dead a number of unarmed demonstrators in Derry. Anger in the Republic of Ireland was intense and justifiable. A group of us happened to be passing the British Embassy when a crowd of protestors set it alight. As we stood and watched it burn, one of the Irish novices put his arm around me in a protective gesture: for them I was not English, but only a fellow-Jesuit.

These two years in the noviceship gave me a rich new set of experiences. Given my circumstances, it was inevitable that the novice-master should become a substitute father; his notorious ill-temper, which coexisted with great holiness, made our relationship a complex one and I was certainly glad when my noviceship ended. This in no way precluded gratitude for the experience – a gratitude that has deepened over the years.

When in 1972 I took first vows, I had more understanding of the Society and a growing sense of 'family' – a family where I belonged – providing that essential support needed during the long round of studies on which I was about to embark. 1972–3 was taken up with philosophy and first steps in Hebrew, a language that has meant much to me on my journey. There is something about the cadences of Hebrew that defeats the translator. Reading the Old Testament in the original languages of those who produced the texts is quite different from working with a translation. Later on, my study of Hebrew and other related languages gave me the privilege of studying Jewish texts with Jewish scholars from whom I learnt much of value about God and the People of God.

For the next three years I studied for the BD theology degree at Heythrop College, (University of London). I worked very hard and thoroughly enjoyed it, though I am aware that my motivation included a good deal of naked ambition. Prayer often goes dry during theological studies, to a point where God seems to have walked out. I was no exception to this general rule, but was helped by the knowledge that prayer, no matter how arid and boring, was somehow a part of who I was.

After these theological studies, I was sent off to teach for a year at a boys' comprehensive mixed-ability school run by the Society in north London. Never having set foot in a non-fee-paying day school, I was exceedingly apprehensive, but this turned out to be a happy year in which I made many valued and lasting friendships among students, staff and parents. It was also an important landmark on my journey in faith, for we used to take some of the students away on retreat to a remote country cottage. I always came back with the sense of having been touched by God, which was a welcome relief after the dryness and doubts of theological study.

This interlude of teaching was followed by two years in Oxford where I studied for an M Phil – an exciting and stimulating period. Then came a year preparing for ordination at Heythrop. I lived in north London and worked with the warm and friendly people in the local parish; for the next couple of years I was a tutor in Biblical Studies at Heythrop, spent another two years teaching at St Aloysius College, Glasgow before beginning my tertianship at Spokane, in the far west of the United States.

'Tertianship', in the Jesuit system, is a kind of international repetition of the novitiate, 'The Spiritual Exercises' and all. It takes place after ordination to the priesthood and after some years of pastoral work. The year is devoted to periods of prolonged prayer, the thirty days of 'The Spiritual Exercises', Society study and pastoral work in a new field. Nowadays tertians are able to choose where they wish to go. I opted for Spokane because Joe Conwell SJ, the tertian-instructor there, had been highly recommended and I liked what he wrote. The Lord gave me far more than I could have anticipated.

For various reasons I was not directed in 'The Exercises' by Joe Conwell but by a former Trappist sister living as a 'hermit' in the city in Spokane; she became a good and valued friend. During this year I also spent two months working with criminal and disturbed boys, and two months working in Guyana where the British Jesuits have a mission. All this and more gave me a deeper sense of what it meant to be a Jesuit, and immeasurably strengthened my commitment to the Society.

The two months with delinquent youth were considered by some to be an excellent preparation for Stonyhurst, my own former school in the north of England, where I became chaplain in 1985. One year later, in front of the whole school, I took my final vows. The boys were amazed that one whom they considered stricken in years, whom they knew had already spent sixteen years in the Society, was only then being installed as a full member: this is the way it had been with the Jesuits since the days of St Ignatius. I was at Stonyhurst for four happy years until I was drawn to my present post at St Joseph's Theological College in Natal, South Africa, where I was to become Superior of the local Jesuit community and teach Scripture.

As I write of these events, memories flood back. Highlights stand out: my ordination, with the joy it gave to my mother, and the tertianship with its fresh and refreshing experiences. I have enjoyed all the work I have been given and all the people with whom I have worked. Furthermore it has been an interesting life and has taken me to Europe, North and South America, the West Indies, Australia and several African countries, not as a tourist but visiting or working with fellow Jesuits. I have been enabled to get close to prisoners, drug addicts, delinquent juveniles, prostitutes and murderers as well as less spectacular characters. I have generally loved teaching and studying. I relish both the vigour and wildness of schoolchildren and the restless intellects of university and seminary students. I have gained more than I can say from my contacts with handicapped and deprived children, while the encounters made through spiritual direction and the sacrament of reconciliation (confession) always leave me convinced of the essential goodness of people.

My occasional work in parishes among everyday folk in London and Glasgow and among Zulus and whites in South Africa have been warming experiences. I have especially valued the welcome received from many families who have shared their joys and sorrows and allowed me, metaphorically, to remove my clerical collar and be wholly myself – a great gift for a celibate.

At this point I am aware of possible impatience. Was it all bland good cheer? Were there no crises? Yes, of course there were. Moreover, on two separate occasions, for reasons that reflect no credit on me, I was glad to be getting out of a place where I had been working. Once, indeed, a crisis seemed so insoluble that I gave serious thought to leaving the Society.

This was when strong feelings of the loss or non-existence of God coincided with a personal relationship with a woman friend. I greatly mishandled that relationship and caused pain to us both. And yet that relationship was enriching and I am grateful for it. I am even grateful for my incompetence although this led to a long wandering in the darkness. On the surface I appeared to be functioning normally, but in fact I was experiencing fearful sadness and bewilderment. At that time I was convinced that there was no God, therefore in performing the functions of a priest, all I could be doing was acting out a charade.

So why didn't I leave? Of course one reason for staying put (and this was put to me fairly forcefully) was the quite unworthy motive of security and status. Maybe, but far deeper was the indelible memory of that midnight Mass at home in 1966, an experience which I could/can no more gainsay than I can deny my own existence. I continued to pray, administer the sacraments and fulfil all the functions expected of priests while it seemed absurd to do so and yet, paradoxically, there were times when I was aware of

God's presence. Once someone who knew nothing of my inner turmoil suggested that I should take one of Carlo Caretto's books for spiritual reading – an occupation which had been obligatory in the noviceship, but which I had long since abandoned. I fell on this book and responded to it like a thirsty plant in a shower of rain.

On another occasion I was praying frantically for X, the lady in question, and heard clearly a voice within me say, 'X is very dear to me.' At about the same time, and often since then, the same voice asks, 'Have I ever let you down?' This always makes me smile and my first instinct is, 'Yes, frequently.' But I know, at the deepest level, this is not true: the Lord has never let me down.

During these bad times, Scripture also spoke powerfully to me. A couple of days before starting the tertianship Long Retreat, I read in the breviary the words of Jeremiah: 'Put yourselves on the ways of long ago; enquire about the ancient paths: which was the good way? Take it then, and you shall find rest.' (Jer 6:16). That brought me up short, for it made me realise that nagging at the back of my mind had been the unformed question of leaving the Society. Was the Lord calling me to a different path? On another occasion I noticed a line in Psalm 110:4 – I had read it a thousand times – 'You are a priest for ever according to the order of Melchizedek.' That came as a deeply consoling word of comfort from the Lord.

And finally, in a convent in Georgetown, Guyana, early one Easter morning, I was flooded with light when I read on the altar cloth: 'Desiderat anima mea ad Te, Deus' (my soul longs for you, O God). Suddenly I realised that in all the darkness those words represented the deepest truth about me. All the time I had been looking for God, God was there or I should not have been looking in the first place; after that nothing really mattered.

This did not immediately solve all problems. In many ways the crisis had not yet fully come upon me. Many of these experiences came when the darkness was still in the future. But from where I look now, I see that moment as decisive. And now darkness has become something of an old friend in my journey of faith. There have been other decisive moments. Happily ensconced at Stonyhurst and fully involved in the work at the school, I was nevertheless aware that I neither could, nor should, spend the rest of my life there. It was then that a letter from a Jesuit friend arrived like a bolt from the blue, asking me to think about joining him in South Africa. I knew beyond all possibility of doubt that this was God's call and that South Africa was where I had to go. In all that followed, an exploratory visit, a retreat in which I prayed for confirmation that the call was the leading of God, the negotiations to find a replacement for me at Stonyhurst and the pain and anger that my move caused, I never doubted that it was to South Africa that God was calling me. Indeed, I remember being disconcerted when someone said disapprovingly, 'Well, it's what you wanted, isn't it?' It was not at all what I wanted, but it was what I knew I had to do.

In my final year of teaching at Stonyhurst I was injured in a skiing accident while on a school trip to the Alps. I was seriously concussed and was unable to work for several months. I still have notes of a 'retreat in daily life' that I made at the time which testify to the bitterness and resentment that I felt because I was neither able to work nor find the key to getting well. I felt that my final year in a job that I loved was being wasted by an absurdity. Now I can appreciate that experience as a blessing – it enabled me to begin to detach myself from a place I loved.

Shortly before I left England, I paid a final visit to Lourdes. It was a wonderful fortnight, and enabled me to say farewell to many old friends. On the last afternoon I spent a very long time quietly in sight of the Grotto and knew that I was content to be setting off on pilgrimage. I had little knowledge of where I was going, but I had the sense that I was going home. So I am calmly joyful to be here, but sad and resentful at the pain it has caused to people I love.

So what has kept me going through all these ups and downs or, put another way, why do I continue to stay? This is a question worth asking for none of us can presume fidelity to the end. For all that, I dare to say that if I were to leave the Society it would be an act of infidelity, given what I have experienced so far. I was talking recently to an older and much loved and respected Jesuit about the difficulties of a man who had left the Society only to find that both his job and his marriage became problematic. 'The older you get,' he observed, 'the more you have to ask, "Am I staying simply because I have nowhere else to go?"' And like many fellow Jesuits I have often heard, 'I wish I had your vow of poverty,' or from a close friend who values the Jesuit vocation, 'Three square meals a day and no heavy lifting,' and such like remarks.

I cannot deny that I am a conformist and am therefore unlikely to change course. Nevertheless, I am certain that I have been called to this way and no other. It is a good way to live and even if God and the Church and resurrection were no more than pleasant myths, being a Jesuit has helped me to grow as a human being. In all honesty I can say that despite a disturbing basic selfishness I have grown in the ability to love over the last twenty-three years. Moreover, the mystery we call God, a mystery at the heart of my being, affirms, 'Yes, this is the right way to live.' I am also aware of a profound and deepening companionship with Jesus along the road.

This sense of companionship is best explained by reference to the twenty-fourth chapter of Luke's Gospel where the story is told of two disciples trudging wearily to Emmaus and failing in their sadness and confusion to recognise Jesus who has joined them on the way. Such has been my experience; a sense that with all the catastrophes, high points, frustrations and mundane routine, my journey is being accomplished with Jesus at my side.

Moreover, I have picked up friendships on the way and these are deeply important to me. Some are nourished by weekly letters; others survive years and thousands of miles in separation, but when we meet we pick up as though we had never left off. Among these friends I gladly include various companions in the Lord, fellow Jesuits and others, and in particular spiritual directors, those companions on whom I have increasingly come to rely. Three of my spiritual directors have been women as have a number of my most valued friends; to them especially I owe a great debt. There are also those friends who are my family: simply by being there they provide an impetus to keep going on the pilgrimage.

I have been asked what developments I would like to see in the Society and the Church. I should like the 'Church', by which I mean the institutional Church, to make better use of the precious gifts of its women members and their sense of the calling of God. I should hope to see it become, thereby, less defensive and more willing to listen. I write these words as one who, in the past, has been afraid of women, but we must slowly learn to surrender this fear. I should also like the power structures of the Church to be seen as structures of service not control. And I should like all of us who are Church to have the openness to learn from the poor and underprivileged. My work in the Society has not, on the whole, been among the poorest of the poor; much of it has been among people from the relatively wealthy background from which I emerged. Here I have discovered the same mix of idealism and humanity as elsewhere, with a very great readiness to respond to ideals once they are placed before them. I have also been privileged in different times and places to see how much we can be taught by the poor, which in my environment means black people and especially black women.

It is clear that the Spirit of God is calling us to learn from the poor. The Church has always had a bias in their favour, but in these days we are invited to let the poor teach us and so help change the way the world is run. It is simply not proper that some should have too much and others not enough on which to live. What is different in our time is that we are learning from the social sciences of sociology, economics and politics about what keeps poor people poor and dehumanises the rich.

As for the Society, I wish three things: first, for a new emphasis on community. In recent years I have learnt the importance of Jesuit community and have a consequent sense of shame for my previous casual attitude. Secondly, I should like to see us rediscover the first Jesuits' sense of mobility for the greater glory of God so that we too are ready to move our creaking bones wherever the pilgrim Spirit calls us. Finally I should like us to get back that sense of risk-taking that so marked our first ten founding companions.

As for myself, I am currently working in South Africa, a country which has given me so much that I am willing to stay for ever. My job is that of helping to form future ministers of the gospel, both Jesuits and non-Jesuits, in the seminary of the Oblates of Mary Immaculate, here in Natal. I teach Biblical Studies and as Dean am responsible for much of the administration. I suspect that forming those who are to lead the new generation of South African Christians in a post-apartheid society may be an important job, given the role the Church plays in this country. The next few years are certain to be difficult, which in itself is an excellent reason for staying. It is an illuminating experience to be living in a society with such obvious injustices. It now seems rather quaint that anyone could ever have defended apartheid; but the injustices here have also opened my eyes to some of the injustices operating in Great Britain.

I enjoy teaching, which perhaps satisfies my need to show off; I also love the study of the Gospels and the attempt to bring them to life for others. But already I have been here for more than four years which is as long as I have spent in any job. I have no idea what the future holds, but I say 'Yes' to it. I have an abiding sense of being on pilgrimage and think I am getting somewhere, but am not sure where; I am sure, however, that I am not travelling alone, that I am making for 'home' and that I shall recognise it when I finally arrive.

Nicholas King SJ
Natal, South Africa

William A. Barry SJ

Born in Worcester, Massachusetts in 1930, William A. Barry SJ completed his schooling with the Jesuits before joining them in 1950. During his formation he spent three years in Germany before returning to the States to study psychology at Fordham University. In 1968 he received a doctorate in psychology from the University of Michigan and the following year was appointed Assistant to the Associate Professor of Pastoral Theology at Weston School of Theology, a post he held until he was appointed Assistant Novice Director in 1985. In 1988 he became Rector of the Jesuit Community at Boston College and three years later in 1991 he became the Provincial of the New England Province – the post which he currently holds. He is the author and co-author of twelve books.

Chapter Three

Towards Integration

In May 1950 Bill Hersey and I were studying for final exams at the College of the Holy Cross in Worcester, Massachusetts. We had grown up in the same neighbourhood and had served Mass together for years. We had gone to different high schools, but in our second year at Holy Cross ended up together in the same classes. At the end of a study session Bill told me that he had applied to enter the Society of Jesus and, if accepted, would enter that summer. I was stunned. Bill had always spoken of becoming a diocesan priest – I was the one thinking of joining the Jesuits, but not yet. As I walked to our family flat, I heard myself saying, 'If he can do it, why can't I?' My parents were in bed, but I told them about Bill and repeated my question. My mother cried; I cannot remember any other reaction of theirs.

A couple of days later I went to Fr Luke O'Connor SJ, who had been my religion teacher in freshman year and had become my confidant and spiritual director. I told him about Bill and, with proper caveats about the strangeness of my motivation, I repeated my question. I had often spoken with Luke about my desire to enter the Jesuits, but I had been in no hurry. I had a steady girlfriend and was beginning to feel confident about my abilities. I remember that a prominent English layman had lectured at the college, prompting me to consider that a married man could do much for the Church and for God. No matter. Within a few weeks I had gone through all the required interviews and had been accepted. Bill and I entered the same day – 14 August 1950.

In the Society Bill and I were not close friends, for some reason that escapes me. About six years after we entered, Bill wrote to me in Germany to tell me that he was leaving.

Almost from the beginning of the novitiate, he wrote, he had suffered from severe migraine headaches. He had often wanted to leave, but had continually been told by superiors to stick it out because he had a 'vocation'. He said that he had almost come to the point of hating God for forcing him to stay. Finally he met a wise Jesuit who told him that God wants our happiness, not our dumb suffering. He was able to leave in peace. I am convinced that if Bill had not told me that he was going to enter the Jesuits in 1950, I would not have entered then. Who knows whether I would have entered? I do not understand this mystery. I cannot believe that God wanted Bill to enter in order to 'get' me. Yet I have at times felt badly that Bill had to go through such suffering, whereas for the most part I have been happy as a Jesuit and now could not conceive of myself in any other way.

Obviously my motivation for staying did not hinge on the fact that Bill was staying. Sorting out motivations for momentous decisions is always tricky. Self-deception lies close to hand, memory tends to fade, chance factors may have more to do with continuing on a chosen path. How, finally, one chooses a particular path is shrouded in the mysterious web of divine inspirations and human intentions, motivations and reasons that largely escape consciousness.

I was born in 1930 in the midst of the depression triggered by the stock-market collapse of 1929. Not that stock markets had much to do with us. My parents were Irish immigrants who had met in Worcester, Massachusetts and had married the year before I was born. Three sisters followed in quick succession. My father was a steel worker, but work was slow during the depression and often broken by strikes. My mother had been a domestic before marriage, but was at home while we were growing up. Ours was a working-class neighbourhood of tenement houses peopled largely by immigrants of whom many were Irish; most of the men worked in the steel mill nearby. On pay-day and at weekends there was much activity at the local bars – violent quarrels sometimes occurred in the neighbourhood or in our house. I think it was then that I learned to use humour as a means of making peace, a trait that stays with me.

It was a relatively poor area, but we did not think much about it. We looked for sales, bought fruit and vegetables late on Saturdays at reduced prices, planted our own garden in the backyard and picked wild blueberries and raspberries which my mother made into jellies and jams. As children we sold magazines and papers. In grammar school I shined shoes, and every weekend I walked four miles each way to a farm to earn a dollar for four hours' weeding and picking. At thirteen I began to work in a fruit shop and continued through high school and my two years of college. I worked thirty to forty hours a week during the school year and close to sixty in the summers during high school – in those days we never gave it a thought.

Looking back I realise that my parents were under a great deal of strain during those hard years, but for all that our house was one of love and laughter and song. Throughout the depression my parents managed to give us a week or two of vacation at a beach near Boston, provided us with a piano and piano lessons and pressed us to do well in our studies. I learnt to study in crowded circumstances and on the run and to endure rather punishing work schedules. I witnessed the generosity of my parents and relatives towards those they loved and those in need; my parents made sacrifices for us children, and my mother and her sister were always sending clothes back to nieces or nephews in Ireland.

Religion was central to our lives; God was an almost palpable presence in our house, and the parish church and school were the centre of most of our social life. We prayed the rosary together as a family each evening, led by voices over the radio. I do not remember when I started going to daily Mass, but by high school it had become a practice. I spent a great deal of time in church activities as a member of the church choir and as an altar boy.

It is hard to recall how I experienced God in those days. In spite of some of the teaching I do not recall being afraid of God or even of being scrupulous. I liked being in church and felt safe there, and lurking on the edges of my memory are feelings of awe and wholeness. I relished the fact that people thought of me as a 'good boy', 'future priest', etc. I also remember that for a time I went to church in the evenings with the hopes of meeting a girl to whom I was strongly attracted. Motivation is a tangled web indeed.

I suspect that the Sisters of Mercy who taught us in

grammar school had much to do with the positive attitudes I had towards God. They were, for the most part, caring, warm and loving women. In addition there were always younger priests in our parish who befriended and encouraged us and served as an antidote to the severity of the first pastor I remember who could strike terror in the hearts of young children. In general I found rest and peace and hope in church and in prayer.

In high school, taught by the Xaverian Brothers, I had my first conscious thought of becoming a priest. One of the brothers asked what I wanted to be when I grew up. Without thinking I blurted out that I wanted to be a priest, but I took no steps to follow up on the desire. Indeed, in my senior year I had made no plans for my future, even though I was the top student of the class. Another of the brothers asked whether I was going to college; this prompted me to apply to Holy Cross, explaining that I could not attend without a scholarship. In August I heard that I had been accepted with a partial scholarship. In my own mythology I put these two questions by the brothers along with the catalytic announcement by Bill Hersey as the seemingly fortuitous incidents that changed my life for ever. Had I not gone to Holy Cross I would not have met the Jesuits and, I firmly believe, my life would have been the poorer.

I suspect that some of the attraction to the Jesuits had to do with the serenity and beauty of Holy Cross. I was impressed by priests walking and reading their breviaries, or talking to one another or to students in the shade of stately trees. There was a feeling of peace and wholeness – that atmosphere was a far cry from the fruit store and my lower-class neighbourhood. Also I had some very good Jesuit professors, men who knew and loved good literature and tried to instil in us the same love of learning and writing well. In my two years at Holy Cross I encountered the best teachers of my life; one, Fr Harry Bean, was nonpareil. I also had a couple of the worst teachers, men with crabbed minds and prejudiced hearts. So my image of the Jesuits was realistic enough. I was impressed by the genuine love of God of a number of these men, and Luke O'Connor was, in my eyes, a holy man who exuded a love for God and his students. Gradually during my first year I began to think of joining the Society.

Motivation? I remember reading a number of lives of saints and feeling drawn by thoughts of being with God and of serving others. The autobiography *Seven Storey Mountain* by Thomas Merton appeared during my freshman year. I read it the following summer and was much impressed by Merton's conversion and call to become a Cistercian monk. I was attracted by the image of finding God in woods and quiet places beside lakes, but I had no attraction to join the Cistercians and still thought of the Jesuits. I did not know much about the charisms of different religious congregations at that time and while I may have been influenced by my desire to help others, my primary motivation was the desire to come closer to God and to be happy – relatively happy.

The Jesuits bought Shadowbrook, a beautiful mansion in the Berkshire hills of western Massachusetts, for a novitiate and juniorate. Two huge dormitories were cobbled together, one for sixty or so novices, the other for the fifty or more juniors. Each novice and junior had a desk, chair and kneeler in a room with up to twenty others. The corridors were lined with sinks to which each of us were assigned for shaving and brushing teeth. Showers were in the cellar and privacy was at a premium. Moreover, much of our life was regimented and governed by fear. Young men, for example, were sent home for having ulcers, one heard routinely that the novice-master had threatened to send men home for failures in the exact following of the regimen. Again we accepted the situation without much questioning, even if at times we wondered at the pettiness of some of the rules.

For all that it seemed idyllic to me when I entered in the summer of 1950 with thirty-six other young men – most straight out of high school. The setting was uncommonly beautiful with the red-tiled roof and stone-and-stucco walls of Shadowbrook, built on a low hill overlooking Lake Mahkeenac. My heart still skips a beat when I recall praying in the hills above the buildings and sensing the closeness of God.

Mind you, most of our formal prayer had to be done in the chapel or in the crowded rooms, kneeling at our desks, always surrounded by others. That formal prayer I remember more as a task than as a pleasure. The prayer we were taught was the meditation form for the First Week of 'The Spiritual Exercises'. We spent forty to fifty minutes each morning at our desks in 'meditation' after which a bell rang to announce that it was time to kneel in prayer, a time called the 'colloquy'. For a long time I considered myself a pretty pedestrian 'prayer' precisely because this formal prayer left me rather dry.

But looking back, I recall times outdoors when I was, quite literally, enthralled with God and the beauty of God's creation. Those times must have sustained me and moved me deeply because I still have vague impressions of specific places and times. Once during a retreat I was walking in the woods above Shadowbrook on a clear, bright day and felt overcome by the beauty around me and thanked God with a grateful heart. I may even have told God at that time that I loved him. I also recall being moved by nature poems; unconsciously my need for contemplation was being fed. Only later did I come to realise that this kind of contemplation was what Ignatius proposed to retreatants in 'The Spiritual Exercises'.

After three years at Shadowbrook, two in the noviceship and one in the juniorate, I was sent to Germany. Our province had a policy of sending a few scholastics to Europe each year for the three-year period of philosophy studies. Fred O'Brien and I were the first to be sent to Germany. Our provincial refused to let us go early in the summer to learn the language, telling us that we could learn the language just as well in the seminary in Weston, Massachusetts as in Germany! This was not the first time I realised that superiors did not have a pipeline to God for wise discernment. We arrived in Pullach on the outskirts of Munich on 25 September; classes began on 1 October and of course we knew precious little German. Luckily the major courses were taught in Latin, as was true throughout the Society in those days. Nevertheless the first few months were something of a nightmare since even times of recreation involved trying to understand and be understood.

For a young man who had only twice been out of the state of Massachusetts, to board a ship for Europe was a heady experience. Before taking the train for Germany we spent a few days in Paris, that magical city to which I returned whenever I had the chance. After Paris, Fred and I took a boat from Koblenz to Bingen travelling up the most beautiful part of the Rhine, with its fabled castles dotting the shore. Paris and the beauty of the Rhine stand as symbols of many wonderful experiences enjoyed during those three years. In Paris I saw many paintings which I had previously admired as reproductions in the library at Shadowbrook. I remember hours spent in the cathedrals of Notre Dame, Chartres, Rheims and Amiens, places where God was a palpable presence. I had read the plays of Claudel and Bernanos; in France I saw them. In Germany I saw plays by Goethe, Wagner's operas and heard both the St Matthew Passion and Beethoven's *Missa Sollemnis* – these were my first live concerts. I also visited the early Jesuit colleges and revelled in the achievements of the Society. On bicycle trips with my best friend Adolph Heuken SJ, now a priest in Indonesia, I found again places of breathtaking natural beauty in the German Alps and with him explored many architectural gems. All these experiences fed my contemplative spirit and broadened my religious horizon.

These cultural opportunities were made possible by a wonderful rector, Fr Glahn, who was a breath of fresh air. Back home our classmates had few such chances to go out of the seminary for cultural or recreational purposes. Indeed, two had been sent back to the novitiate as a punishment for seeing a movie in town. Fr Glahn only lasted two years as rector; rumour had it that he was too easy going as a superior. His successor, Fr Georg Trapp, was also a man of openness and breadth of mind. He was a psychologist under whose direction I wrote my thesis on Jung and it was he who planted the seeds of my future interest in psychology.

I was in Pullach from 1953–6, a time before Germany's 'economic miracle' was complete and when bombed-out buildings and partially-restored churches were still in evidence. Some of my classmates were veterans of the Second World War: one man had lost some of his fingers, another's face had been restored by plastic surgery and others had experienced bombing raids while in school. I do not know what effect this had on my attitude to war, but now my initial reaction to the thought of war is one of revulsion. During those years the

German Jesuits had to live on modest means; once again, as had happened when I was a child, I found that I hardly noticed that we were poor. I seem to be able to make do with whatever circumstances life presents and have the sense that God will provide – an attitude that comes in handy in my present job as provincial.

During my years in Germany, I studied philosophy with some brilliant and demanding teachers who taught me to think critically. I also became interested in modern psychology, especially the psychology of C. G. Jung; for my final thesis I wrote on his theory of personality types for which I read almost all his works. I was fortunate enough to make a retreat directed by Karl Rahner SJ, the great philosopher and theologian. I became intrigued with his thought and during this time began to read his philosophical work; he has been a strong influence on my thought and spiritual life. As a result I began to put more credence in my own experience as a source of contact with God. During these years I also became acquainted with the work of Hugo Rahner, Karl's brother, who wrote on Ignatius and Jesuit spirituality. I began to conceive of the marriage of modern psychology, spirituality and theology, a theme that has dominated my subsequent life in the Society. I could already read French fluently and could now read German – a great help. The rather bizarre notion of sending me, proficient in French, to Germany, while sending another scholastic, proficient in German, to France, has paid off in my life. God writes straight with crooked lines, as the Portuguese proverb has it.

In 1956 I returned to the States to teach Latin, English and German at Fairfield Preparatory School in Connecticut, which I thoroughly enjoyed and wanted to continue. During my second year Fr James Burke, the Province Prefect of Studies, visited Fairfield and asked me to spend my third year of regency studying psychology. I told him that I liked high-school teaching and that if everyone who was good at it went on for higher studies we would have few good high-school teachers, but a few months later he convinced me that it was in the best interests of the province for me to study psychology. As a result I spent the third year of my regency earning a master's degree at

Fordham University – as it turned out this year sealed my future work.

While at Fordham a chance discussion revealed, to my surprise, what was going on in my heart. One evening a group of priests and scholastics were debating the merits of the vow of chastity. As the discussion progressed, I got increasingly impatient with the arguments for the vow of chastity, most of which seemed too utilitarian. I could not say of myself that I was more available for others than my parents, for example, or than many dedicated lay people I had met and worked with at Fairfield. Finally I blurted out, 'I'm a Jesuit because God wants my happiness, because being a Jesuit is the best way for me to be fulfilled, and God knows that.' Just as I surprised myself when the Xaverian Brother asked me what I wanted to be, by blurting out 'A priest!', so too in this incident. I had no idea that this conviction was in my heart. Yet to this day I believe in the truth of those words. Just as Mr Liddell, in the film *Chariots of Fire*, believed that God made him fast and delighted in his running, I believe that God delights in my happiness as a Jesuit.

After the year at Fordham, in which I learnt the fundamentals of psychology and did a thesis on the testing of candidates for the Society, I began the study of theology at Weston College, another country place west of Boston. For the next four years, 1959–63, I studied theology there and was ordained to the priesthood in 1962. My ability to read French, German and some Spanish enabled me to get an excellent theological training, while in Scripture studies I wrote papers on the Holy Spirit in all the books of the Hebrew Bible and in St John's Gospel. At that time I had my first two articles accepted for publication in *The Bible Today* and was encouraged by some of my professors to consider seriously further study in theology. However Jack McCall, the wise Jesuit and psychologist who had advised Bill Hersey that God was no ogre, was urging me to pursue psychology with the idea of replacing him at Weston College. I decided that many of my contemporaries were very able in theology, but I was the only one who was also proficient in psychology. Furthermore I was still intrigued by the thought of wedding psychology, spirituality and theology, so I agreed with my superiors to pursue a doctorate in clinical psychology after

I had completed my tertianship. The die had indeed been cast when I went to Fordham in 1958.

My tertianship, which preceded my doctoral studies, was significant both because of my experience in making 'The Spiritual Exercises' and because of the community of Jesuits with whom I lived. This was made up of men from my own province, from various parts of the country and the world. During 'The Spiritual Exercises' I remember telling Jesus that I loved him, the first time that I had such a strong personal relationship with him. Since then this relationship has grown closer and deeper. During the year we tertians formed a close-knit community. We shared our experience of prayer and ministry, we discussed the meaning of religious life, and especially Jesuit religious life in the post-Vatican II era. We became self-confident in our own commitments to the Society and had the sense that the future of the Society was going to be in our hands. Not all of us remained Jesuits, but for me that group had a great impact on my future as a Jesuit. I felt committed not just to Jesus, but also to those other companions of Jesus, and through them, to other Jesuits I would meet in life. These commitments carried me through the heady and challenging years that followed.

During this year, almost by accident, I decided to study for the doctorate in clinical psychology at the University of Michigan rather than at Harvard University. It was a last-minute decision, swayed by the reputation of the psychology department at Michigan. Thus, instead of moving to Cambridge, Massachusetts and a settled Jesuit community, I went to the small university city of Ann Arbor, Michigan where the twelve or more Jesuit doctoral students lived in rooming houses and took meals at the local Catholic hospital. We had to create community if we wanted it. And we did. Once a week all the Jesuits would get together for dinner. In my second year four of us rented a house and began what may have been the first 'small' community in the country. We learned to cook for ourselves and our house became a focal point for regular gatherings of the Jesuits in Ann Arbor. Moreover, the community became more open; a daily 5pm eucharistic community developed at St Joseph's Hospital chapel, attended by most of the priests and religious studying in Ann Arbor. On Saturdays a rather large group of men and women religious gathered for Mass and a pot-luck dinner and sharing. We became a group of close-knit friends in the Lord. A number of the friendships that developed there have been life-long, even though we are separated geographically.

During these years many of us religious rediscovered the importance of the opposite sex in our lives. We had to learn how to relate in depth with women and men and yet remain celibate, and we had to learn without much training or experience. Most of us had entered religious life as teenagers, and our formation had not given us any help in developing close relationships with persons of the opposite sex. It was an exciting, challenging and painful time. A number of the religious in Ann Arbor in those years of the middle to late sixties decided to leave religious life and to marry; a number of us recommitted ourselves to the religious life. None of us emerged from these years unchanged. For myself I believe those changes were for the better and I look back on that time with great gratitude to the community of men and women who struggled with me. I am well aware that motivation is a tangled skein and that I remained a Jesuit throughout those years and beyond through a mixture of dumb luck, fear of what people would say, of uncertainty about making a living, fear of committing myself to one person for life, etc. But I also choose to think that my commitment to Jesus, to my brother Jesuits and to the many people to whom I ministered played a role, and indeed the strongest role in my motivation to remain. As I look back over my life since Ann Arbor, I find that I have no regrets for missed opportunities. Indeed, I find that I have been more alive, more full of zest for the Jesuit life and more fulfilled. I attribute the happiness of my life to the grace of God which brought me to Ann Arbor and which kept calling me to live out my life as a Jesuit.

In those years of the late sixties we faced heady social issues such as the Vietnam War and American militarism, racism and social injustice. We were all involved in one way or another in the turmoil produced in American society by these and other issues, but my main occupation at this time was the study and practice of clinical psychology. I became rather a good clinical psychologist and researcher and was asked to remain on as lecturer and researcher at the University of Michigan, after I had finished my dissertation on conflict in marriage and personality patterns. During that year I came to the conclusion that my heart was not in the university department, but in the religious community; I was not cut out for life as a professor in a secular university. I decided with my superiors to return to the province as a counsellor and professor of pastoral theology at Weston School of Theology, which had just moved from the country estate to Cambridge, Massachusetts. Here I finally arrived at the integration of myself as a Jesuit, a psychologist and an apostle.

Before Vatican II, preparation for priestly ministry was almost entirely cerebral, with little pastoral training beyond practice in hearing confessions and celebrating Mass. There was hardly any attempt to help us to relate our experience of God to our ministry and when I was first ordained I was sent as a chaplain to Boston City Hospital for a month. I had an intellectual conviction that God was present to sick and dying people, but I was scared stiff and did not know how to talk to people about their experience of illness. I relied on the dispensation of sacraments to justify my presence on the wards. I do not recall that I experienced God's presence during my ministry at that hospital; I believe that I was too self-concerned to mediate God's presence. As I look back to that first experience as a hospital chaplain, I realise that my own deepening relationship with God was somehow divorced from my ministry.

Preaching was a different story. There I believe I was able to bring experience to bear on a gospel text and speak to the real lives of people. However, as a clinical psychologist in Ann Arbor and even when counselling Jesuit seminarians at Weston School of Theology I never asked myself how God was present in the experiences my counsellees spoke about. My clients, even Jesuit clients, did not speak of their relationship with God in their therapy. The situation was put very clearly by a Jewish psychologist, one of my professors at Ann Arbor, who had been trained as a psychoanalyst in Europe. He said that if religion is a neurosis, as Freud believed, then religious experience should be analysed just as any other experience. Yet in psychoanalytical literature one never reads of 'religious' experiences being analysed. In his early years as an analyst he had had an orthodox Jew as a client. After some weeks the client gave up his treatment saying that it was threatening his religious beliefs. At the time my professor interpreted his action as resistance to treatment. Later on, however, he became more relaxed about his own religious background and more open to the realm of mystery and faith. He told me that his patient's reaction was, at least in part, a valid reaction to his therapist's own ambivalence towards religion. As he became more at ease with mystery and religion, he found that many of his patients brought up religious issues in their therapy. Not only that, but the patients of those he was supervising also spoke more often of religion. He concluded that the absence of the mention of religious experience in analysis was due, at least in part, to the counter-transference of the analyst. What amazes me now is that this very interesting discussion did not make me wonder about my own clinical work in which religious experience never made an appearance.

I believe that I had neatly compartmentalised my life so that religion and psychology only intersected in theory. In my research on conflict in marriage I had developed a theory of interpersonal relationships and I was interested in applying this theory to the spiritual life. But it was not until the early 1970s, when the compartmentalisation of my own life began to break down, that I began to realise that all experience could have a religious dimension and that this religious dimension also required my attention as a psychologist.

A group of us Jesuits began to train ourselves to give 'The Spiritual Exercises' to individuals, in the manner originally intended by Ignatius. Out of these sessions came the decision to found a centre dedicated to research and writing on the spiritual life, to the training of spiritual directors, and to the provision of spiritual direction to anyone who could profit from it. The Centre for Religious Development opened its doors in 1971, and I found myself devoting more and more of the time previously given to psychological therapy, to the work of the Centre. Theology and psychology began to intersect in practice.

At the Centre for Religious Development we took an empirical approach to the spiritual life and used the methods of clinical supervision in the training of spiritual directors. We were interested in people's experiences of God and discovered that they wanted to talk about them. I was fascinated by the stories people told about their inner life even as I also became aware of something in me and in them that resisted the closeness to Mystery. We developed a definition of spiritual direction as that form of pastoral counselling whose purpose is to help another to develop consciously his or her relationship with God and to live the consequences of that developing relationship. We focused the sessions of spiritual direction on a person's experiences of God and the developing dialogue with God that resulted. We discovered that gradually most of the significant parts of a person's life and work were touched upon and illuminated by such a focus.

In this kind of spiritual direction people began to notice more and more inner experiences which they interpreted as the 'voice' or presence of God revealing God's attitudes and values, and they noticed their own reactions to these experiences and were able to tell God about these reactions. They learned in practice how to discern the 'spirits'. Their prayer became more of a dialogue and their lives took on more meaning even if they were filled with pain and sorrow. In spite of the pains and sorrows of life they knew that God was really with them, was their Abba as much as Jesus' Abba. Many also found their lives more challenging and exciting as they responded to Jesus' call to radical discipleship. In this kind of spiritual direction I had found a way to become more integrated in my life and ministry.

The integration consists in a melding of my personal, theoretical and pastoral interests. For all my ambivalence about God, I have since childhood been captivated by the pull towards union with the Mystery we call God. Before I knew about Ignatius of Loyola and 'The Spiritual Exercises', I was using his methods of contemplation, using my senses and imagination to discover God. In my own experience I somehow encountered God and gradually began to trust my own discernment. Moreover, I want others to know God as God wants to be known. My interests in intrapersonal (within the person) and interpersonal (between persons) dynamics find an outlet in exploring the relationship of individuals with

God and also exploring the relationship between the spiritual director and directee. In addition I can use all the skills I learned as a clinical psychologist to help people meet their God and develop their relationship with God. Experience and theory intersect and mutually influence one another. My own love of and desire for union with God come into play in this fascinating ministry. Of course, this ministry also reveals my blindness and resistance to the deepest desire of my (or anyone's) heart, namely to be united with the Mystery we call God, the perfect community we call Father, Word and Holy Spirit.

I have come a long way since Bill Hersey's announcement provoked the question, 'If he can do it, why can't I?' As I look back over the forty-three years since that fateful day, I see that my motivation has been mixed and changing. The one constant has been the desire for union with God and, perhaps, the desire to help others to know that deepest desire of the human heart. I thank God for all that played a part in my entrance and staying and consider that God's calling and God's desire gives as fulfilling a life as possible. I only regret that my own resistance and cowardice have kept me from reaching the full measure of happiness God has in mind for me. But what I have is enough indeed.

Why do I remain a Jesuit? I *am* a Jesuit; that is my identity. I am a sinner called to be a companion of Jesus. I find in Ignatian spirituality and in the Jesuit way of life my way to God. Moreover, I find companionship and friendship in the Society wherever I go in the world. I also find in my brother Jesuits, for all their warts and moles, men who want to know Jesus in order to love him more and follow him more closely.

Finally I find my call as a Jesuit confirmed by close friends who are not Jesuits and by many people to whom I have ministered as teacher, preacher, director and writer. Chiselled into the facade of the Dinand Library of the College of the Holy Cross are words from St John's Gospel: 'Ut cognoscant Te solum deum verum et quem misisti Jesum Christum.' (To know you, the only true God and Jesus Christ whom you have sent, (Jn 17:3)). In the Society of Jesus I have come to know and love the one true God and Jesus whom God has sent and by the grace of God I have been enabled to help others to the same knowledge and love. What more could anyone ask?

William A. Barry SJ
Boston, USA

Cecil McGarry SJ

Cecil McGarry was born in 1929 in the county of Galway in the west of Ireland. He was educated by the Jesuits and joined the Society in 1946. He followed the traditional programme of training and taught for some years before serving as Provincial of the Society of Jesus in Ireland (1968–75). He was then transferred to Rome where he was a General Assistant of the Society until 1983. Since then he has been teaching Theology at Hekima College, the Jesuit School of Theology in Nairobi. He is also a visiting lecturer at the Catholic University of Eastern Africa.

Chapter Four

Seduced

Born in Galway in the west of Ireland in 1929, I lived in various cities of the Republic – Dublin, Limerick, Kilkenny, Dublin again and Waterford until I left home to enter the Jesuit novitiate in 1946. Ours was a conventional home in which religion was important but rarely discussed and never forced. We did not pray together, not even a common blessing at the table. Both my parents and a grandmother who lived with us were daily communicants and as I grew older, I followed their example. Parental affection was strong but not demonstrative. We were three children. I had an elder brother and a younger sister; another brother who followed me died very young.

The idea of a life given to God's service was attractive from an early age. I had been struck by the dedication, friendliness and happiness of the Jesuits I had known in Belvedere College during the three years my brother and I were at school there (1939–42). Some of the priests in my parish in Waterford provided fine examples of what a good priest could be and do. I had found James Brodrick's *Origin of the Jesuits* in the public library in Waterford and was greatly attracted by the spirit of the early Jesuits described there. Vague at the time about what I wanted from life, I only knew I wanted something worth while. The little I knew about the Jesuits seemed to offer possibilities. I applied and was accepted. I think I knew instinctively that my parents would be happy for me to become a priest, though they never indicated it, unless by helping me to achieve it when I said that this was what I wanted.

A few months short of my eighteenth birthday, I set out for the novitiate, at that time situated at Emo Park, former home of the Earls of Portarlington, in the midlands of Ireland. There, in a very short time, I found my heart and mind captured and my idealism given focus during the month-long 'Spiritual Exercises' of St Ignatius. Before finishing them I was certain that I was in the right place and I had already developed a sense of belonging in and enthusiasm for the Society of Jesus through an identification with the Ignatian vision of companionship with Christ in mission. The ideal of striving for the 'more', the 'greater', which I was beginning to understand as central to the Jesuit grace, offered abundantly the something worth while I was seeking.

My first crisis was altogether unexpected. I developed a painful back condition which was diagnosed as a tubercular abscess on the spine which would require prolonged treatment in an orthopaedic hospital. The doctors made it clear that I would not be strong enough for Jesuit life. Suddenly I was no longer a Jesuit novice. My disillusion was complete and I was deeply rebellious against a God who seemed to be playing games with me. How could he give me a vision of life that had captivated me and now throw me aside? I never suspected that I could be capable of such strong rebellion as I felt in the first weeks of lying strapped to a frame in Cappagh Hospital. A bitter inner struggle followed. The nun in charge of the ward, seeing me so sorry for myself, kept challenging me to be a man and to live up to the ideals that had been mine in the novitiate. I bitterly resented her words at the time but afterwards recognised the part she played in bringing me through this crisis.

Slowly, over a period of about three months, the realisation dawned painfully that the heart of my novitiate vision had been a companionship that required a radical availability to God and his will. Reluctantly I came to see that God could be calling me to live that availability to him as a layman and possibly with impaired health for the rest of my life. It was one thing to understand that this was the real meaning of what I had committed myself to during 'The Spiritual Exercises', quite another to accept it now in quite changed circumstances. I could never forget the moment I did so, during a sleepless night in Cappagh Hospital. It was a moment of great pain but profound consolation in which I accepted that my life was God's gift to me and that it was for him to determine its course; my part was to be available to his will. The real meaning and demands of the words of St Ignatius' First Principle and Foundation, which had deeply impressed me during the long retreat, were suddenly clear to me:

> It is necessary to make ourselves indifferent to all created things. . . . Consequently, on our part we ought not to seek health rather than sickness. . . . Rather, we ought to desire and choose only that which is more conducive to the end for which we are created.
>
> Sp.Ex. 23:5–7.

Not just to accept, but to desire and choose! I knew then that this was the real meaning of the 'election' I had made during the long retreat: availability to God for Jesuit life was not enough, it had to be an availability to whatever he might ask. Ever since, I have known that the grace of that intensely painful yet deeply peaceful moment must remain for me the criterion of every choice I am faced with in life. It has been an uncomfortable grace to which I have not always been faithful.

The next X-rays showed the abscess cleared and such was the surprise of the doctors that they had them repeated. What had happened? Had the original diagnosis been faulty? Had the blessing with the crucifix once owned by the saintly Jesuit, John Sullivan, been effective? I did not know. Nor did I desire to know, since those months had been so fruitful in such an unexpected way. I was profoundly grateful. A painful period of physiotherapy, convalescence and readjustment at home preceded my return to the novitiate where I was greeted by the novice-master's sentence of doom: 'Brother McGarry, you will begin *ab ovo*' (literally, from the egg). That and the months that followed in the novitiate gave me my first experience of what St Ignatius calls the confirmation of the election (Sp.Ex. 183:1–2). Though repeating the novitiate was very difficult, I retained a deep inner peace and a sense of the rightness of what I was doing.

After that I followed the then traditional Jesuit programme of studies, beginning with three fruitful years taking a degree in English and French language and literature at University College, Dublin. They were followed by three years of scholastic philosophy at the Jesuit Faculty near Tullamore in the Irish midlands. Though it should have been an intellectually stimulating time, it was not so for me. I did not feel challenged by what was offered, though I did learn to think more clearly and to try to face problems honestly. To follow the truth wherever it leads became an idea and I was convinced that truth always liberates. During the years of philosophy, I began to make a personal study of 'The Spiritual Exercises', and found their pedagogy fascinating. Another important moment at this time was taking the Rohrshack test[1] with the professor of practical psychology, which resulted in a growth in self-knowledge and, much more important, in self-acceptance. When afterwards I was able to integrate what I learned about myself into an acceptance of God's unconditional love, I experienced a considerable growth in inner freedom.

The two years I spent after philosophy as teacher and prefect in a Jesuit boarding college, since closed, were both happy and brought their own crisis. It was wonderful to be active and in a position to discover many potentialities that had lain dormant during the years of study. But in my inexperience and arrogance, I judged the college was poorly run and seemed not altogether to correspond with Jesuit ideals. Could I spend my life in a place like that? Did I wish to? I realised that obedience could require it. These questions remained with me during the two years and I only found peace in the Exercise on Two Standards during my annual retreat at the end. Yes, I would be ready to spend my life there since the way of Jesus Christ was that of poverty, humiliation and humility, but I would have to do everything in my power to improve it. This was a step forward in learning the meaning of availability in practice and how to live Jesuit ideals within the imperfection of the human condition. In this state I moved on to the Jesuit Faculty of Theology at Milltown Park, Dublin, to begin my final period of study and to prepare for ordination to priesthood.

These were the last years of the old theology and I found it for the most part turgid and not very interesting. I was disappointed. Another disappointment was the election as

Pope of Angelo Roncalli, a seventy-seven-year-old cardinal of whom I had never heard. I had been hoping for a man who would open our church to new things. I was happy very shortly afterwards to acknowledge how wrong I had been in my judgement of John XXIII!

Before ordination my provincial told me that I should do further studies, a doctorate in what he grandly called mystical and ascetical theology at the Gregorian University in Rome, to prepare to be master of novices. I took advantage of the summer months after my final exams in theology to go to Paris where I stayed for two months, one in a suburban and one in a city parish, helping with masses, confessions, etc. The rest of my time I spent reading Ignatian spirituality and sources at the Library of the Review Christus by day, while frequently at night I was in the cheap upper galleries of the Comédie Française or the Opera, where I enjoyed much of the classical French theatre and opera for a pittance. It was a great summer, the joy of which was not obliterated even by a letter from my provincial a few months later while I was in tertianship at Rathfarnham Castle, Dublin, telling me that plans had to be changed and that I should proceed to Rome at the end of my tertianship to take a doctorate in canon law.

I must admit that my spirit of freedom and availability for any service was sorely tested. Canon or Church law held no interest for me and the last thing in the world I wanted was to spend my life teaching in a seminary. By this time I had become interested in all aspects of Ignatian and Jesuit spirituality and was looking forward to further studies and a life devoted to working in this field. The by now familiar struggle for inner availability began again and long before it was over there was a further change in destination, which came this time from the Visitor whom the Superior General had sent to the Irish province with extensive powers to review its life and ministries. He told me I was to go to Rome in September to prepare to teach systematic theology, in particular the doctrine on the church. He did not want any discussion; the matter had been decided. I was filled with all kinds of conflicting emotions: relief that canon law was off the menu, dejection at the thought of a life to be spent teaching in a seminary, for which I felt neither capacity nor interest. A complete acceptance did not come easily but it was helped by the short-term prospect of being in Rome during the Vatican Council. Already an atmosphere of theological excitement was widespread throughout the Church.

I arrived in Rome on the eve of the opening of the council, 10 October 1962. The memory of the following morning has remained vividly with me ever since, when with a great throng of faithful in St Peter's Square I watched some 2,000 bishops precede Pope John XXIII into the basilica to open the council. Instinctively I knew I was witnessing history in the making. The following day I was very moved on reading John's opening address to the council in which he affirmed that the Church's mission was to enter into dialogue with the world, to listen to its questionings and have confidence that the gospel can bring light and some answers, adding that the message of revelation was one thing, the way it was formulated today another.

I think my vocation as a theologian was born in those early weeks of the council through Pope John's compassionate, non-condemnatory and dialogical approach to the world. The Church no longer seemed monolithic and immovable but was described by John as a servant community in relations of friendship with all, which must take account of the signs of the times. I found myself identifying deeply and warmly with these sentiments, which I was hearing for the first time. During the two following years I was working for my doctorate at the Gregorian University but renewing and learning theology at the many conferences given all over the city by the world's greatest Christian theologians, present in Rome as expert advisers to the bishops or as observers from other churches. I began to be more aware, too, of the human face of the Church as I discovered the intrigues and politics of the council.

I left Rome in mid 1964, enthused by what the council was doing and believing that theology could be not only interesting but even exciting. I was happy now to be called, as I thought, to give my life to it. In 1965, my first year of teaching, another wonderful event took place: the charismatic Basque Pedro Arrupe was elected Superior General of the Society of Jesus. This was to affect my life much sooner than I realised. Three months later the Rector of the theologate was appointed Provincial, responsible for the Society in Ireland by Father Arrupe, who also named me to succeed him as Academic and Jesuit Community Rector at Milltown Park. The meaning of availability again became a stark reality. I knew the appointment had come far too early. I was without experience and taking my very first steps in the way of becoming a professional theologian. I was only a few years older than the sixty or so students and very much younger than all the members of staff, all but one of whom had been my teachers. In the bout of insomnia that followed, fear was about equally mixed with hopes and dreams of what it might be possible to do.

In the community my hope was for greater openness, sharing our vision of faith and Jesuit life together, moving from formal to more personal relationships, from an authority to be obeyed, and sometimes feared, to one that sought to serve the responsible freedom of the members. Needless to say, I soon came up against our common fragility – my own and that of others. But we did take first steps together, steps that were altogether too short and mincing for some of the younger members, and for others held the menace of enormous strides beyond the known and the safe.

It was clear that if the academic institution was to follow the lead of Vatican II, many changes had to take place. Like the Church, it would have to reach out beyond itself if it were to give what a school of theology seemed called to give to the Church and society in those years. At that time each clerical congregation in Dublin had its own house of studies with its own staff. I asked myself why we should not work together, share facilities, share teaching skills and experience, share ownership and responsibility and thus bring our students together in a wider and more challenging environment. In this way the Milltown Institute came into being through the openness and enthusiastic support of many of the religious superiors. For some years there had been an outreach to lay people through the series of Milltown public lectures initiated by Father Michael Hurley whose personal contribution appears in this volume, and whose enthusiasm and courage were a great support in those years. We now attempted to share with the religious sisters some of the fruits of the Vatican Council and their response was enthusiastic. Milltown began to be enriched from outside and continues to expand creatively, celebrating in 1993 twenty-five years of service as the Milltown Institute of Philosophy and Theology.

I only became fully aware of the depths of what I myself received from the Milltown community and academic institution when I was abruptly moved at the end of three years as Rector. I had experienced warm companionship with many as well as the great difficulty of moving from what has become traditional. I learned much about leadership, sometimes painfully, at other times in the happiness of discovery together. It was insufficient preparation, however, to take up the office of Provincial to which Father Arrupe called me in July 1968. I was unready for this appointment and so were the members of my province, who were not expecting a change of leadership and had not been consulted. I was largely unknown to them – except probably as the one who had changed so many things at Milltown, hardly a felicitous recommendation!

How does one describe six and a half years of intense activity as Provincial, trying to implement the new directions, not always easy to discern in practice, called for by Vatican II and our own thirty-first General Congregation? Besides, Pedro Arrupe was challenging us to distinguish between the mission of the Society in any given province and its actual works. They might have coincided in the past; we must ascertain whether they still did so today. Through his famous 'social survey' carried out in every province of the order, he was asking us to review our way of life and mission. It was my responsibility to ensure that the findings of the survey in Ireland were implemented.

The Irish province had many long-established and largely very successful ministries, especially its secondary schools. It was difficult for many members to understand why these institutions should be asked to question themselves. It was – and I acknowledge it gratefully – the very dedication and generous commitment of the province members to their works, together with the inadequate theology (for a new situation) which they had learned, and the limited knowledge we had of our own dynamic sources of life, 'The

Spiritual Exercises' and especially the Constitutions, that made evaluation and change so difficult. Were we not doing good things? Undeniably. But were they the better things? Were they the most needed in Ireland at the time? Were they serving the more universal good? Were they the works that others were not doing? Fidelity to our own Constitutions and to Pope John's signs of the times required that we ask such questions. Pedro Arrupe's convictions and vision had become mine.

I often failed in communicating that vision to the province members. I lacked expertise and patience. I was coming to them out of the spiritual experience of the renewed theology and vision of Vatican II and out of my enthusiasm for the courageous insights of Pedro Arrupe, which they had hardly yet had the opportunity to share. I was inept and untried. I knew I was causing much pain to older and more experienced men who had been in the ministry before I joined the order. My constant temptation was to withdraw, to give up, to blame others for not seeing what to me seemed evident. But even then I knew it was not so evident. If it had been, and if I could have conveyed it, most would have followed. I often asked myself, 'Why should you have to go through all this? Why should this burden be laid on you? If people do not want to move forward, why wear yourself out?' At the end of every struggle of this kind I recognised the evil spirit of self-pity, of lack of perseverance and lack of love. Ignatius loved his men, so did Arrupe. How could I learn to love more and to persevere in love?

My lowest point in these years was the Provincial Congregation of 1970, the first I had attended, and which I had to lead. I saw it as an opportunity for taking a big step forward and went into it with some trepidation but considerable hope. As I experienced it, however, it turned out to be largely a looking backward rather than forward, a resistance to change, a defence of the status quo, a desire to see the arrival point clearly before taking a first step into the unknown. We seemed to be so full of fears of the changing world and wanted to cling to security in the known and the well-tried. I felt that love was being suffocated by fear and that we were unable even to admit our fear to one another. If we could, perhaps we might move forward.

During the congregation and afterwards, I was over-whelmed by a deep desolation and discouragement, a sense of personal incapacity and helplessness. Could I continue? Why should I continue? What right had I to try to lead people where they did not want to go? And I had to admit that I was not sure where they should go. But I wanted us to search it out together and discover it in the process. It was difficult to pray in this desolation. Indeed I didn't want to pray, because I suspected that prayer would lead me to the inevitable surrender to a God who can ask of me what he wants. This time I did not want to say yes. I had had enough. And this time it wasn't only a matter of interior surrender, I was filled with doubt that I was the one who could lead at that time. I felt I would do more harm than good if I were to try to move forward in what I was convinced was the Jesuit way. I had failed so far. But I was not willing to betray my convictions or my mandate from the Superior General.

After much reflection and some consultation, I began to think that there might be another way. Would it be possible to facilitate new spiritual experiences among us that would free us from fear, help us to communicate together at a deeper and more personal level, and so enter more fully into our Jesuit grace? I decided to go to Rome to talk with Father Arrupe and share with him my tentative thoughts on a new way forward. I also told him that if he did not think it was good or if he felt he could not back it, I would prefer if he were to put someone in my place. I was greatly strengthened by his understanding, his insistence that I continue, even if what I proposed would also fail. Thus began a series of communication workshops, individually directed 'Spiritual Exercises', unknown in Ireland at the time, and sessions of Ignatian spirituality and the Constitutions, all led by Jesuits from other provinces, who were generous in coming to help us. We began to be able to talk to one another more freely and many grew greatly in inner freedom and an ability to share our Jesuit ideals. Many became free enough to become pilgrims like Ignatius, allowing God to lead them where he wished.

Then I judged the province was ready to look at itself and its works through the eyes of a wonderful Christian layman, also skilled in organisation and management, who visited the communities and met all those who wished to speak to him. The openness to him could hardly have been greater, and he was able to write a perceptive report in which the members of the province recognised themselves, and in which he offered many recommendations for a better and more participative running of the province. These were well accepted. Through the friendship, encouragement and competence of this layman and those with whom I worked in the new structures, many things were achieved that would have been unthinkable just two or three years before. There was still misunderstanding, of course, and reluctance to change but the sails of the lumbering galleon began to catch the wind and it slowly began to move forward. I still failed to communicate a vision well and know that some who might have become more open could not do so under my leadership. I regretted that at the time and regret it still today.

My inner effort in those years had to be to remain faithful to the call of the Church and the order and not to let a desire for approval or popularity turn me aside. One paragraph of 'The Spiritual Exercises' formed the main theme of my prayer. The most recent English translation calls it 'The third way of being humble'; I have always thought of it as the third way of loving:

In order to imitate Christ our Lord better and to be more like him here and now, I desire and choose poverty with Christ, poor rather than wealth; contempt with Christ laden with it rather than honours. Even further, I desire to be regarded as a useless fool for Christ, who before me was regarded as such rather than as a wise and prudent person in this world.

Sp.Ex. 167:3–4.

My poverty was my inability to share well what I believed to be the vision of the Church and the order. I was not shown contempt but I did have to cope with criticism. There were those who thought me lacking wisdom and prudence. I could not say they were wrong. There were also those who encouraged me and without whom it would have been difficult to continue. These were years of grace in which I began to find God more easily in the many things, situations and persons I had to deal with. St Ignatius calls this 'devotion' (Aut.99; Cons.282,528). I think I came to know what he means.

There is insufficient space here to write of the other areas of intense activity during those years. I refer to the efforts of Religious together through the Conference of Major Religious Superiors of Men, of which I had been elected to the chair, to seek a renewed service of the Church in collaboration with bishops, priests and lay people. We discovered together the meaning of the Church as a communion. Again it was an enriching and consoling experience even if it was not also without contradictions and oppositions. They were years of friendship, support and encouragement from many in the Irish churches which enriched me humanly and spiritually. Many of these friendships continue today. There was also work with individual religious congregations in the sphere of renewal. Ecumenical work was just beginning in Ireland at the time. They were years when the members of other churches often showed more enthusiasm for church unity than was apparent among us Catholics. It was they who made ministry in this area possible and very rewarding.

My life took another abrupt and unexpected turning during the thirty-second General Congregation when I was elected one of the General's four Assistants *ad providentiam* – and became counsellor and companion in his government. I had gone to the congregation with a conviction that it must give provincials and the whole order the clearest possible guidance on apostolic priorities for the years ahead. I hoped it would have the courage to reform the legislation of St Ignatius on the grades (see Glossary) in which members belonged to the order, some as solemnly professed priests (a minority over the centuries), others as helpers in the spiritual sphere (see Glossary), others again in the temporal, the brothers. I was convinced that, while this made sense in the time of Ignatius, it no longer did so. I feared, however, that we might not have the courage to face the issue. But members were ready for these and many other issues.

These were the two, however, which created problems in the Vatican. This is not the place to chronicle our difficulties with the Holy See during the congregation itself. At one point, Pope Paul VI wrote an autograph letter to the General saying that we should not have discussed the question of grades at all, expressing doubt about some of the orientations emerging from the work of the congregation and asking, 'Is the Church able to have faith in you here and now, the kind of faith it has always had?' He asked to see the decrees of the congregation before they were published. History will evaluate in due time all the events of these years. What is clear, however, is that Pedro Arrupe and the order did not have the confidence of the central authorities of the Church during the remaining years of his generalate. There were also those within the order who had no confidence in him, in his government or in the orientations of the thirty-first or thirty-second General Congregations, especially the commitment to a service of faith which saw the promotion of justice as an absolute requirement. Some of these had the ear of high Vatican officials.

Working closely with Pedro Arrupe was a great grace. He gave me the special responsibility of overseeing the formation and studies of young Jesuits throughout the order. He also asked me, in accordance with the mandate of the General Congregation, to take charge of the review of the functioning of our central government and administration. In this latter I was not successful. Organisation and management are taken for granted as part of life in the Anglo-Saxon world but are less appreciated in the Mediterranean world, where we were situated. Some small improvements resulted – but they were small. This was a painful but instructive introduction to my life and work at the General Curia, the Society's central office in Rome. It lasted about a year, during which I was also making contact with the world of Jesuit religious and intellectual formation, and indeed with the Church worldwide. This part of my work was a joy through the years that followed. I was able to meet young Jesuits and those in charge of their formation in parts of the world that I had previously only heard and read about: Africa, India, East Asia, Latin America, with their cultures, theologies and ways of spirituality so rich and diverse among themselves and so different from all that I had known. I think I was able to bring them something of my enthusiasm for our common vocation and leave them with a sense that their particular situation and way of living that vocation, with all the difficulties and challenges involved, was appreciated and to some extent understood at the centre. As I moved around I discovered how much Pedro Arrupe's leadership meant in the whole order and how deeply he was loved by so many.

It was a difficult time to be an assistant. During the years of Pedro Arrupe's generalate up to 1981, when he suffered an incapacitating stroke, he set the Society firmly on the road of Vatican II and re-expressed the heart of its spirituality in terms of the twentieth century in a series of documents that constitute a rich spiritual heritage. But he did so in a climate of increasing unease in relations with the central authorities of the Church. Personally I lived those years in a conflict of loyalties between what the Spirit seemed to be saying to the Church and the order in council and congregations and what the Institution was saying and doing. A movement of restoration was taking a firm grip in the higher echelons of Church government and towards the end of the time seemed to be firmly in control, with some notable exceptions. Twelve years on there is still lip service to Vatican II and its vision, but is it more than that?

This is not the time or place to chronicle the difficult and painful ending of the Arrupe generalate. After the General Congregation had elected his successor towards the end of 1983, I was asked if I would consider going as Dean to the new African theologate in Nairobi, in the planning of which I had been involved, and which was due to open in September 1984. So began the present stage of my call and response. I have found a new home in Kenya and its church, which has welcomed me and opened for me the possibility of using much of the experience that has been accumulated over the years. It has been wonderful to return to the teaching of theology, though I am very conscious of my limitations as an expatriate, and to have had a part in the creation of Hekima College (*hekima* means 'wisdom' in Kiswahili), this new theological centre for the Society of Jesus in Africa and Madagascar, and helping to create links between it and the new Catholic University of Eastern Africa, with its centre in Nairobi. It has been a privilege to accompany some of the local religious congregations in their search for growth, depth and stability in times of political, social and cultural transition in Kenya, and even to accompany the founders of a new one. None of these religious, I think, could guess how much they have enriched me through their deep religious spirit and their human qualities. It is also a privilege to be able to offer some service to the church in Kenya as it prepares for the Synod on Africa in 1994, and to share in its pain that the synod will not be held in the continent.

The pain and inner struggle of the Arrupe years and the years since have centred for me around the question: how does one put all one's energies and enthusiasm behind bringing to realisation the vision of Vatican II while in the Church one loves and serves many seem to be working in the opposite direction? The removal of Pedro Arrupe and his appointed vicar and the placing of the Society of Jesus under a papal delegate is only one example among many. Many of the most burning issues in the Church community are resolutely excluded from the agendas even of synods of bishops by papal authority. Are the bishops not to be trusted? What is the true meaning of collegiality? Should we not search for truth, wherever it leads, confident that it will set us free? Truth about such issues as the place and role of women in the Church, sexual morality, obligatory celibacy of the clergy in the Church of the West, the demands and limits of collegiality and inculturation. . . . Is there no danger that we are forgetting the stricture of Jesus, 'You load on people burdens that are unendurable, burdens that you yourselves do not move a finger to lift' (Lk 11:46)? Is open dialogue, so treasured in the early Church and by Vatican II, to be entirely abandoned? Why do we not believe any more in the guidance of the Holy Spirit, but only in that of central authority? Is this the way to foster loyalty, participation and love within the Church? Is this the way the Church of Rome should preside in love over the whole community?

What Elspeth Huxley wrote of Africa in *The Flame Trees of Thika* may be applicable to our Church today. 'Africa,' she wrote, 'is a cruel continent; it takes your heart and grinds it into powdered stone – and no one minds.' I have not found this to be true of Kenya, where I have lived now for nearly ten years. Moreover, in the Church there are also those who mind. But these last years have been cruel to those whose hopes were raised by Vatican II and to those who have given themselves wholeheartedly to that vision in faith, loyalty and obedience.

How does one continue to 'feel with the Church' and to love it – such integral aspects of the Jesuit way of life – when the Spirit of Jesus seems to have been arrested and confined, as Jesus himself was in his time? No, let me ask rather the only question I can answer: how do I continue to love this Church? My response can only be in the truth so well expressed by Blaise Pascal many centuries ago: that the heart has reasons about which reason knows nothing. Over the years I have discovered that love only truly becomes love when it has been tested and proved by its own defeat. I think the humiliation of Pedro Arrupe was the moment at which I experienced this most deeply and was able to express it to myself in words. Many of the things I hold dearest seem to be trampled under foot today – and those who should, do not seem to mind. I have frequently felt defeated, my heart ground to stone. But I know that love can and must transcend defeat and only then does it truly become love. So I love Christ in this Church because I cannot love him apart from his Church. He lives in this body, in which I too am a sinful part. I have learned slowly to love even in darkness because not to love is to deny my own being. I have been made for Love and by Love. The truest human moment of love for Jesus was that of his defeat. Ignatius has asked his followers to try to learn this way of love, the Third Way (Sp.Ex. 167:3–4).

I make the words of Jeremiah my own: 'You have seduced me, Yahweh, and I have let myself be seduced; you have overpowered me! you are the stronger' (Jer 20:7). The Lord seduced me in my hospital bed in Cappagh many years ago. I have often been unfaithful and with Jeremiah have said, 'I will not think about him, I will not speak in his name any more,' but each time the Lord has been the stronger. Experience through the years has taught me what Ignatius meant when he wrote that one should be intimate with God in prayer and in all one's actions (see Cons.723). My deepest moments of intimacy with the Lord have always been in the struggle to remain available to him, faithful in moments of darkness, defeat, frustration, weariness, in the big and small rebellions of every day when I have tried to impose my wisdom and my ways. I continue to find him more intimately when he proves stronger in the daily demands for availability and service than in times of prayer. I find God more sensibly in the things of every day which require effort and surrender of self than in times of formal prayer which are often 'empty' and dry, lived in faith and the natural feeling of wasting time. Ignatius' note in the 'Exercises' which can appear cold and negative has become positive for me and an experience of 'devotion': 'For everyone ought to reflect that in all spiritual matters, the more one divests oneself of self-love, self-will and self-interests, the more progress one will make' (189:10). The Lord's companion, Peter, discovered this, and with him I too can only say, 'To whom should I go? You have the words of eternal life, and I believe. I know that you are the Holy One of God' (cf Jn 6:68–69).

Endnotes

1 A psychological tool in which the making and interpreting of inkblots plays a prominent part.

Cecil McGarry
Nairobi, Kenya

A. Patrick Purnell SJ

A. Patrick Purnell SJ was born in Wales in 1923. He was educated at a boarding school run by the Jesuits and joined the Society himself in 1941. He followed the normal pattern of Jesuit training and taught for some years. In 1967 he went to Motherwell, Scotland as the Bishop's adviser on Religious Education and from 1980–7 held the post of National Adviser for Religious Education to the Bishops of England and Wales. He has written several books and is currently writing on justice spirituality. He is also a much-valued spiritual director.

Chapter Five

Late Developer

I live in a terraced house in Brixton which I share with a group of young Jesuits from a number of different countries who are studying theology at Heythrop College, London. I spend my time listening to people who come to me for spiritual direction, writing on justice issues and helping people in groups to reflect on prayer and justice by giving weeks of guided prayer, etc. I enjoy this kind of life and remain a Jesuit because the Society of Jesus supports and enables me to be myself and to do just what I am doing. But this is not all, the Society has been the means of my reaching the present point in my journey because the Society itself has been on a journey these past decades – a journey with which I can identify. It has been discovering what its basic charism, finding God in all things, means in our world today. In this journeying, the Society has perceived that the struggle for faith necessarily includes the struggle for justice and that to be alongside the poor is to be in a privileged place where God is to be found. Lest the reader think that s/he is about to read what we used to call a *pia fabula* (a nauseatingly pious yarn), I want to add that in some respects I am still a Jesuit in spite of the Jesuits.

If I had been struggling to tell this story twenty-five years ago, it would have been very different. Had I been writing then, I would probably have talked in terms of the fear of infidelity, of being true to one's call from God and, perhaps, of the imperative of proclaiming the gospel. The latter, thank God, is still on the agenda, but the focus of my life has changed significantly and so today I tell another story. I am a late developer and a slow one! I only discovered Ignatius and 'The Spiritual Exercises' after thirty-seven years of Jesuit living and then, not at the hands of a fellow Jesuit, but through the patient insights into myself and 'The Exercises' of a sister of Notre Dame (Kathleen McGhee). It was in the flat lands of East Anglia that I began to get in touch with my 'feeling life' and to learn to value it for what it is, the place where 'the Creator and Lord in person communicates God's self to the devout soul in quest of the divine will' (Sp.Ex. 15).

'The Spiritual Exercises' of Ignatius are the life-blood of the Society of Jesus; they provide the raison d'être and dynamic of its existence. From my earliest days in the Society, the 'making' of 'The Spiritual Exercises' was an integral part of life. However, over a long period this 'making' had drifted away from the approach of Ignatius and his companions. When I first made the full 'Exercises', I had to listen to five talks a day: there was little time or energy left for prayer. The retreat had become an in-service training in Jesuit spirituality and this methodology was not seriously questioned until the late sixties and the early seventies when the original insights of Ignatius into the relationship between the retreat director and the one making 'The Spiritual Exercises' began to be recovered.

As I slowly came to understand 'The Spiritual Exercises' I discovered two important things. First, that they provided me with a way of discovering a goal, a vision which would endow me with a dynamic to govern and motivate my life; secondly, through making 'The Exercises' a dream began to emerge. I believe in dreams. The dream is the attraction, the energy, the dynamic – call it what you will – which grapples with the possibilities of who you are and what you want to be. It is the motivating force of what you do and how you live, no matter how much and how often you fail to do and be what the dream dictates. At times there seems little connection between the 'now' – the immediacy of the day's doings, the flow and intricate tangle of events, and the goal – what is yet to be. But unless the dream is in place, unless one believes that the 'trivial pursuits' of one's unexciting, hum-drum, banal existence contribute in some measure to the accomplishment of the dream, one is left with a world without meaning. Somewhere along the line of my life I made my own a sentence of the philosopher

Michael Oakshott, 'To be human is to live in a world of meaning, to be without meaning is to be a stranger to the human condition.'

Why am I still a Jesuit? Because within the marrow of Jesuit life I discovered that the essence of religious life, the essence of being a Jesuit, is a constant search for meaning for my life and for the world in which I live. I learnt the art of dreaming and I named a dream for myself. The dream speaks of the Kingdom which Jesus proclaimed in terms of the transformation of society; it speaks of a world in which people live together in peace, truth, justice and love sharing the earth's resources; it speaks of God's choice of the poor – God's choice of me – as God's coequal partner in the shared mission of creating a new order of love. God chooses the poor not because they are more virtuous than other people – they are not necessarily so – but simply because they are poor and banished to the edges of human company. What binds God to act, as it were, is not human virtue but human need. God is totally God in responding to the cry of the needy and the poor.

Secondly, I discovered through the insights of Ignatius that it was all right to be myself. This was a question of handling my own self-image. The fruit of the initial stages of 'The Spiritual Exercises' is the gift that a person comes to know with absolute conviction that s/he is the loved and forgiven sinner; it is the sinner forgiven and continuing to be forgiven who is chosen by Christ to be his companion in bringing into being the reign of God – the transformation of society. It is only within this understanding of God's absolute, unconditional and gratuitous love that the sinner can cope with her/himself. 'The Spiritual Exercises' offer me a spirituality which has enabled me to cope with myself, uncomfortably at times, and has taught me the importance of journeying – of being a pilgrim. The Society of Jesus has provided me with the context in which I can be a pilgrim and embark on a pilgrimage on which I have not been allowed to get holed up in one particular watering place but have had to move on, remembering that the horses get restive; the pilgrimage is not a sinecure – Jerusalem beckons.

A dream! A way of being myself! As I come to tease out the history of the pieces of my life which come together to

tell of that dream and which have enabled me to be myself,
I seem to be in touch with a pattern as I let memory recover
the times, the places and the circumstances of the journey.
No – pattern is not the word. Pattern implies a too intelligible
meaning at any given point; what I am in touch with is more
like a tune of four or five notes, sometimes played softly by
a solo violin, sometimes by the whole orchestra resounding
in the believing fabric of my life. At other times, the tune is
difficult to identify amid the embellishment of the brass or
in the deep-throated motif of the double bass. Nevertheless,
it is persistent – a Pied-Piper tune inviting my sluggish feet
to follow. It is a melody in which I am attuned to myself and
to God.

I can trace a faint resonance of this tune in a remembered
exhortation delivered by a retreat-giver who, quoting Car-
dinal Newman's 'Never grow old to God!', told us that
although we might not then understand, it was vital for
our spiritual growth that we should not decline into senility
in our relationship with God. But the tune was initiated
by a number of talks given by Tom Corbishley SJ during
a Triduum (three days of prayer) towards the end of a
novitiate which had not been exceptionally noteworthy for
its insights. Tom Corbishley developed his thoughts on
'What does it mean to be a Christian' around those words
in the Mass: 'through him, with him and in him' which
immediately precede the 'Our Father'. To be a Christian
is to be in Christ! His words fell like rain on parched land.
Subsequently, during philosophy I read A. Wikenhauser's
Pauline Mysticism, making copious notes. Until then, Paul's
'and it is no longer I who live, but it is Christ who lives
in me' (Gal 2:20) was no more than the basis of a pious
prayer suitable for Holy Communion. However, despite the
fact that my spiritual life (though I doubt whether I would
then have attributed to myself anything so grandiose as a
spiritual life!) was being nurtured by these ideas, I was at
the time wholly engaged in a war in which there was neither
remission nor a foreseeable end.

To understand this conflict I must go back to the begin-
ning. I bumped into the world of the twentieth century at
Coryton on the outskirts of Cardiff in the early years of
the twenties. It was a time when the experiences of the

First World War, in which my father and my uncles had all fought, were being assimilated. The year of my birth heard America broadcasting to Britain over the radio for the first time and saw the first Labour government assume office; Hitler was in prison after the failure of the Nazi putsch at Munich, writing *Mein Kampf*, the blue-print of Nazism. And, more personally important, the Irish civil war broke out following the acceptance of Dominion status the previous year. Michael Collins, the Irish leader, had been assassinated and the Hallinans, my mother's family, were in uproar, being fiercely Irish. Grandfather Hallinan, so family legend has it, spent one night in Shrewsbury jail, having denounced Queen Victoria at a public meeting.

My first school was called 'Vaucluse'. The Misses Parker, from Australia, had turned their bungalow into a private school for children up to the age of eight. There I learnt to read and write, to add and subtract, to multiply and divide, and to master my catechism and the intricate process of saving my soul. It was from this classroom that we were marched, two by two, to make our first confessions in the local parish church, a few minutes away. We had all been drilled to examine our consciences rigorously and to confess our sins clearly so that 'Father' could hear and understand us and validly absolve us.

If at that time I had asked the younger of the Misses Parker how I would know if I had sinned or not, she would have replied that I would have no problem because when I examined my conscience each night, the wrong things I had done would make me feel guilty – this meant that God was not at all pleased with me. What I then had to do was to make an act of good contrition, which admittedly was very difficult, but it did make God happy with me again. Then I could go safely and happily to bed with the added bonus of a smiling Guardian Angel looking down on me. Had I pursued the subject, which would have been unthinkable as I was of a meek and unquestioning disposition, and asked what happened when I discovered no sins to make me feel guilty, I would have been asked whether or not I had included pride in my self-examination. There was no way, so it seemed at that time, of relating to the rather daunting deity except around the axis of guilt. There was, it is true, a period after making a good confession and having my sins properly forgiven and my penance said, without distractions, when I knew that God was happy with me and everything in the world was all right, but that period was only too brief before I plunged myself once more into a life of sin.

For me the situation was intensified by two factors: the tension within the family and the tension within myself arising from an abnormally pious disposition. Long prayers said without distractions around my holy pictures were part of my nightly ritual; I believed they would keep at bay the divine displeasure and prevent my small world from disintegrating. This was not to be. Before I had reached the age of eleven the depression of the thirties struck and my father lost his job. Relationships worsened and soon afterwards the uncles began to appear in the house. I was banished to the kitchen, with my younger sister, where there was no wireless and I could not continue to listen to a fascinating serialisation of a Victorian melodrama called *Vice Versa*. Solemn negotiations were going on in the front room. My parents' marriage was at an end. A bachelor uncle on my mother's side, who ran the family business, moved in to assume financial responsibility for the home and for our education. My father went away and I saw very little of him ever again. I had failed. I had not succeeded in keeping the divine displeasure at bay. The questions I had wanted to pose to Miss Parker about what happens when one doesn't feel guilty never came up again until I buried my growing years in an evening sunset. In those days all I could do was pull up my sleeves and redouble my efforts to keep the divine wrath at a manageable distance.

Before my father left home, I had been moved from the intimate setting of my small scholarly bungalow to the rough world of a boys' preparatory school. There I found myself struggling not only to keep on the right side of the divinity, but also in the good books of my teachers – a more immediate and terrifying task. The deity in his infinite wisdom had created a slow learner and had not seen fit to share with him the divine ability to spell.

Protestants indulged 'in the private and personal interpretation of Scripture'. I am not sure exactly when this riveting piece of theology entered my consciousness, but it did so at a very early age. Neither am I sure exactly what I made of it at the time, but whatever it was it must have sent a shiver down my Catholic spine and persuaded me to keep away from Scripture altogether and from a too personal involvement with the God of those sacred books. I already had some experience of that God to reinforce my argument. There was actually very little chance of my falling into the cardinal error of private and personal interpretation because the Scriptures were, after all, Protestant and we did not read Protestant books. Good Catholic teaching instilled in me the need to keep my head down: say my prayers without distractions, go to Mass and confession and keep myself pure and unspotted from the world – and all would be well. It was not until my third year in religious life that I actually read a Gospel right through. Nowadays it seems extraordinary that a person can go through the Thirty Days' Spiritual Exercises of Ignatius paying so little attention to the Bible.

With the coming of the uncle into the family home, I was sent away to the boarding school which he and his brothers had attended. I cannot say I enjoyed the experience and it is a wonder that I hitched my life to the Society which ran it. There I began to pray the rosary with great fervour to ward off the temptations of the flesh, and I began to head daily for the confessional; this was, after all, the God-given means of keeping oneself pure and unspotted. Only an élite have had the facts of life whispered in their ear through the confessional grille before half-past-seven Mass in the morning! It is difficult to diagnose exactly what was happening to me at that time so long ago. Suffering from a sense of inadequacy and loneliness, I had begun to find comfort in a strange fantasy life which continued to disturb and trouble me. Perhaps ill health had something to do with it – I had a rheumatic heart which had kept me at home for a full term.

During our final years at school there was great discussion among those of us who 'had a vocation' as to whether or not we should join the forces and 'go to war'. Going to the novitiate was deemed to be what God wanted of me, and because I was not considered to be very bright, I left school the year before I was due to enter Rhetoric (sixth form), and began my Jesuit life at St Beuno's in north Wales in 1941. I was to be at St Beuno's for four long unbroken years, without spending one night outside the house. Looking back with fifty years of journeying behind me – years of revolutionary changes in church and Jesuit thinking, what happened or rather did not happen within those hallowed walls is almost unbelievable. It was the end of an era when ritual not only held liturgy in thrall but pervaded every facet of life and created its own demanding rules and regulations. We were not being offered a formation; instead we were subjected to a process in which we had to do naught but submit as the Jesuit grid was lowered onto our persons, knocking off the undesirable, unwanted and unreliable pieces of our character. The war was raging fiercely while we clung to the side of our Welsh hill and learnt how to conduct ourselves as religious, according to the manner of the monastic tradition, even though we were never intended to be monks. The novitiate day was designed to accustom us to a rigid routine and was hedged in by a series of petty rules and regulations contrived to wean us from our secular existence. Great emphasis was placed on silence and on acquiring a modest and religious behaviour. Very little attention was given to study except the study of piety and the Constitutions of the Society. The human had to give way to the supernatural.

The juniorate followed the novitiate and it was there that I was introduced to the mysteries of higher mathematics. I studied philosophy at Heythrop (Oxfordshire), then had three very happy years teaching in north London at St Ignatius', Stamford Hill, followed by a year in south-west London at Manresa, Roehampton where I acquired a teaching certificate, then back to Heythrop for theology and on to priesthood.

I enjoyed theology and it was during those years of study that I gradually realised that I was not as dim as I had come to believe. I found that I was able to think for myself and began to do so. At the end of philosophy many of my contemporaries had been sent to Oxford to do a degree. I had been judged not to have the aptitude which was not particularly helpful to my self-image and reinforced my lack of self-confidence which had already been undermined during the painful years of school and juniorate. In theology, however, I slowly found myself picking up certain major themes and making them part of my reflective life. I put it this way because at that time I had no real understanding of what was meant by the spiritual life. The tune played gently, evocatively. Thinking back to those years I now realise that I had very little sense of who I was. I had spent my years trying to measure up to the image offered me of what it was to be a Jesuit. I had put my energies into making myself fit into the Jesuit mould; adjusting myself to what I perceived as the Jesuit archetype. I believe the power of this dynamic absorbed me in my approach to the priesthood. Being a priest was part of the Jesuit package, a very important part but nevertheless a part of something which was more dominant and demanding. There was no doubt that I wanted to be a priest, to celebrate Mass and to exercise a priestly ministry, but I am not sure that at the time I came to terms with what priesthood really was for me. Today, in a church struggling to redefine itself in so many areas, the ambiguity persists. I am a priest and I know my priesthood to be an essential part of my identity; I cannot but be a priest. Somehow it sets me in a particular relationship of service to my fellow human beings. Nevertheless, over the years, for the most part, I have not exercised a sacramental ministry; my ministry has been rather that of the word – a ministry, some would argue, which could be exercised equally well by one who has not been ordained. That is the dilemma! It would take me far beyond the scope of this particular piece of writing to explore and set out the implications and arguments involved in this.

At the end of 1956 I returned to St Beuno's for tertianship. I once more made the Thirty-Day retreat. It was still being given according to the traditional pattern with many conferences and little contact with the Master of Tertians who was giving 'The Spiritual Exercises'. I made the retreat with great fervour; here was the chance of a lifetime; the last chance, perhaps, to conquer myself. The retreat ended and at Christmas I broke down. I retired, haunted, to Heythrop. My fantasy life had got the better of me and plunged me into a world of deep depression. It was not until the spring that the then spiritual father, Kevin Booth SJ, suggested that perhaps I might benefit from seeing a psychiatrist. My first session with Dr Elkisch was somewhere around

Easter, and a dozen years had to elapse before my final session.

The psychiatrist's couch is the place where all is revealed! Doctor Elkisch did not have a couch; I sat opposite him in a comfortable chair and, over the years, facing the sensitive and understanding doctor, I dug deep into the seed bed of my consciousness and uncovered the tangled roots of my emotional life which had created such horrendous guilt and so deep a depression. For years, perhaps twenty-five or more, I had sidled furtively into the confessional, morning after morning or night after night, to confess impure thoughts and imaginings. I was plagued by these images so I plagued my confessor. My only hope then was that one day I might learn how to overcome myself and conquer them or else that they would miraculously disappear. During our years of training, confession was always on tap. There was no problem in going into 'father' each night, kneeling down, saying one's piece, always the same, receiving one's penance and getting absolution. I am amazed today that I was able to get away with it. Yet what I was doing was symptomatic of the kind of spirituality then acceptable. One had a duty to keep oneself pure and in a state of grace; this was the era of the spiritual he-man!

In September 1957 I was sent back to north London to teach at Stamford Hill again. Living in London meant I could keep up my weekly appointments with Dr Elkisch. I enjoyed teaching, mainly elementary mathematics and religion and I became deputy headmaster. I remained until 1965 when a fairly momentous change took place. I left the classroom and took up 'catechetics' beginning with a one-year course at the newly-opened Corpus Christi College in London. It was a tremendous year. Vatican II was percolating into the veins of theology and Karl Rahner was our guru. It was a heady time. Christ had risen – and in his rising had breathed his Spirit into my life! The whole orchestra played the melody, loud and clear. It changed my life. My visits to Dr Elkisch were less frequent although I was to continue to seek psychiatric help for a number of years. Clouds of depression still came down upon me and the confessional was still my valium. Nevertheless, new ideas and the new spirit gripped me.

The year of catechetics at Corpus Christi was followed by

my appointment to the diocese of Motherwell in Scotland as an adviser in religious education with the late Tom McGurk, a priest of the diocese. That was in 1966, the year that I met Bet, and I was to remain in Scotland for the next eleven years.

I have a problem with the phrase 'falling in love'; 'falling' has something precipitous and violent about it whereas I experienced something slow and gentle. 'Love' is not a static concept but something changing, volatile, many faceted; it is a 'doing' word rather than one expressing a state or a situation. Love is a journeying with all the qualities of a journey: excitement, exploration, unknowing, trusting, joy, laughter, sadness, tears and difficulties. It engenders its own impatience, pains and sorrows; its highways and byways; its struggles and the long piercing beauty and peace of companionship. I met Bet and I began to love her although I never matched her love for me which was totally overwhelming and gratuitous – never sparing, never holding back: 'You will never know how much I love you!' It was a love which accepted me as I was with clear, compassionate eyes; accepting me as man with my distortions and bouts of depression stemming from my bizarre imaginative life, and as Jesuit and priest. It was this love which slowly taught me what it is to be a human being; what it is to love, honour and value myself – in a word, to be human! Bet was human with an incredible gift for laughter: 'I never laugh so much as when I am with you.' The glory of God is a human being fully alive and I was beginning to find the gratuitous, all-pervasive love of God. Bet could accept me as I was; and there was no longer any question, 'Could God accept me?' Since Bet did, so did God. The verbs I use are in the past tense. Cancer began to work its way through her body; she died on the last day of May 1988, during my sabbatical year.

Scotland proved to be a time of learning in more ways than one. What I had studied and reflected upon during the previous year at Corpus Christi had to be translated into the language and culture of the home and the classroom. Some parents and teachers welcomed and were excited by the new approaches to religious education; others, fearful of losing the structures which held their religious world together, attacked the innovations with vigour. What they wanted was 'solid doctrine' not this 'airy-fairy' nonsense about loving God and loving your neighbour. As an adviser in religious education I led an embattled existence and became absorbed in the work. I enjoyed writing extensively for both primary and secondary schools. I gave talks to parents and teachers and visited schools day after day. The thrust was catechetical; it was centred on developing a relationship with a living and loving God rather than on handing on a series of articles of faith. And our methodology lay in trying to root all that we taught in the experience of our audiences.

In the course of this work I heard once more and unmistakably the melody which quickened my steps. The music came to me in a passage from Colossians:

> I became the servant of the Church when God made me responsible for delivering God's message to you, the message which was a mystery hidden for generations and centuries and has now been revealed to his saints. It was God's purpose to reveal it to them and to show all the rich glory of this mystery to pagans. The mystery is Christ among you, your hope of glory! this is the Christ we proclaim. (Col. 1:25–28).

The mystery is Christ in you. In religious education I was not trying to give Christ to anyone but to help others to discover Christ within them; to help them to be aware of Christ's life.

Towards the end of 1978 I moved back to St Beuno's for a period of about eighteen months. During those months I gave the 'Thirty Days' Spiritual Exercises' in full four or five times, on one occasion at Guelph, in Canada. I became gripped by the concepts, the images and the dynamic the 'Exercises' initiated. God accepted me just as I was in my messiness and loved me with a love beyond my wildest imagination. Christ invited my inadequate and crippled self to work with him in his kingdom. It was at this time that the melody came through clearly and penetratingly in the ideas of a fellow Jesuit, Michael Ivens. The resurrection as contemplated in the fourth week of 'The Spiritual Exercises' can be considered as an education in a new form of presence. Those to whom Christ showed himself came to understand

'Christ within me'. The risen Christ was feeling his way into the farthermost depths of my being. Then I really began to come to terms with discernment. Throughout my life I had been over familiar with the destructive forces pent up within me. Now I began to name and love the life-giving forces of the Spirit and their movement within me. At last I had found an answer to the question I never asked Miss Parker nearly fifty years previously, 'What is happening when you examine your conscience and you don't feel guilty?'

My stay at St Beuno's was all too short. At the beginning of 1980 I assumed the grand title of National Adviser for Religious Education to the Bishops of England and Wales, a post I held for seven years. I suppose the two most important pieces of work in which I was consequently involved were, first, the introduction of the Rite of Christian Initiation for Adults (RCIA) which involved organising the first RCIA Summer School. And, secondly, the initiation of the National Project.[1] The latter involved me in writing *Our Faith Story* which has proved a useful tool in helping teachers and parents to understand the changes which have taken place over the years in religious education. The book caught the music and the melody clear echoed at the heart of what I wrote. God in Christ is present everywhere within our reality and is to be found in the most unexpected places.

> Our first task in approaching another people, another culture, another religion, (another person), is to take off our shoes for the place we are approaching is holy; else we might find ourselves treading on another's dream. More serious still, we may forget that God was there before us.[2]

I was also struggling to express the validity of personal experience in the story handed down to us by our Christian forebears; struggling to honour my experience as the place where 'the Creator and Lord in person communicates God's self to the devout soul in quest of the divine will' (Sp.Ex. 15) and trying to respect the experience as much as the story. I was reclaiming 'my catechism and the intricate process of saving my soul' and discovering that it was not so intricate after all. I was setting the doctrinal tradition within the mystery of God's goodness, within the heart of God's gratuitous, never-ending love for humanity and the presence of Christ in our reality. I was in the process of freeing myself at last from the rigidity of a doctrinal expression which imprisoned my spirit and appeared as something alien within my experience to which I had had to bend my mind and my will. The story which I received from those who have gone before me points the way and guides me to a deeper understanding of the mystery of God.

I am still a Jesuit because of a dream. Being a Jesuit has enabled me to be myself and to continue to search for that self. The dream is in place; the search goes on. I am still a Jesuit because that tantalising melody which has doggedly pursued my steps plays more persistently around my sluggish feet now I have reached my three score and ten years. As I listen to that tune of four or five notes, I find still hidden within it the same question upon which Tom Corbishley reflected fifty years ago, 'What does it mean to be a Christian?' and I find myself still trying to answer that question. But now I realise that this question which continues to challenge me today is the question which we, as a Jesuit body, are constantly asking ourselves.

Because the Society belongs to this world, it must ask this question, because the very raison d'être of the Society is summed up in finding God in all things. This is the Jesuit charism which dictates to those who espouse it a search for God. I am taught to pray in the 'Contemplation to attain the Love of God' at the end of 'The Spiritual Exercises' that 'I may in all things love and serve the Divine Majesty'. In all things! In recent General Congregations which epitomise the working out of the charism of the Society, considerable stress has been placed on justice as a constitutive element of faith and on the Society making an option for the poor. To be a companion of Jesus today is 'to engage, under the standard of the Cross, in the crucial struggle of our time: the struggle for faith and that struggle for justice which it includes' (Gen. Cong. XXXII). 'Similarly, solidarity with men and women who live a life of hardship and who are victims of oppression cannot be the choice of a few Jesuits only. It should be a characteristic of our communities and institutions as well' (*ibid*).

I cannot separate myself from the world in which I live or from the crucial struggle of our time. I am compelled to strive to be in solidarity with men and women who live in hardship, oppressed by a world in which the remorseless tide of capitalism relentlessly absorbs resources to the exclusion of the poor. I am aware of the power, privilege and wealth of the few and of the teeming millions of the poor and the oppressed pushed against the margins of the world. In consequence, I have to ask myself, where is God? Where is God for me? And ask too, what is justice? What is this privileged place which the poor occupy and which is so special to God? What is meant by the option for the poor? What does it mean to identify with Jesus Christ who identified himself with the destitute, the homeless, the famished, the banished, not because they were good or holy or virtuous – they were no more virtuous than the rest of society – but because they were victims as he was to be a victim. How do I find him living and acting through the power of the Spirit at the heart of the problems and struggles of the poor? These questions emerge as important issues; they are not nice speculations but arise out of need, out of my own poverty and out of my own journeying 'to find God in all things' and my struggle to make sense of myself and the world in which I live.

Why am I still a Jesuit? What else can I be?

Endnotes

1 The National Project of Religious Education was initiated in 1985 under the auspices of the Bishops' Conference of England and Wales. It was envisaged that an agreed programme of religious education would be produced beginning with preschool children and continuing into adulthood.
2 A. Patrick Purnell SJ, *Our Faith Story* (Collins: London, 1985) p.92.

A. Patrick Purnell SJ
London, UK

Peter Knott SJ

Peter Knott SJ was born in 1926 in Essex in the south of England and educated at a local grammar school. In 1943, during the Second World War, he enlisted as a private soldier and was later commissioned as an officer in the Royal Artillery and posted to the Far East. After the war he graduated from the Staff College, Camberley and served in Palestine, the UK, Germany and Norway. In 1962 he was received into the Roman Catholic Church and joined the Society of Jesus shortly after taking early retirement and leaving the army. Since completing his training in the Society, he has been an airport chaplain at Heathrow, Religious Superior of the Farm Street Community in London and is currently the Roman Catholic chaplain at Eton College. He paints as a hobby and has exhibited his work on three occasions.

Chapter Six

Where I Belong

The First World War had ended a few years before, everyone was preparing for the General Strike, and I was born. 1926 was as good a year as any other in which to start life. The future was unknown of course, but what was totally unexpected was that in 1964, at the age of thirty-eight, I would become a Jesuit novice.

It took me just about all this time to become a Catholic. My parents were baptised in the Church of England and although I cannot remember ever going to church as a family, my brother and sister and I were sent to Sunday school as children, but this left no conscious impression. My mother had been so upset by the minister's indifference when my brother was baptised that she refused to present my sister or myself for baptism later on. Religion played no formal part in our family life, but the love and example of my parents were formative in a way which I can only now fully appreciate. With their encouragement I won a scholarship to the local grammar school and there a boy introduced me to a Bible class. I didn't care for the hymns but I did like the look of the girls, and so I joined the summer camp which was run on evangelical lines. I began to pray every evening, just talking to God, not quite sure what I was doing but feeling that this was right for me. After a year or so this phase died away, and I thought no more about religion. Then in December 1943, when I joined the Army as a seventeen-year-old recruit, the Sergeant asked, 'Religion?'

'Well, er, not sure. . . .'

'Cee-erv-Eee.'

Thus I acquired 'honorary' membership of the Church of England along with my Army number.

Later I was commissioned into the Royal Artillery, and after the war in the Far East was offered a Regular commission. In 1942, when I left school, I had worked briefly as a management trainee in a large industrial firm but this had not caught my imagination. Service life seemed to offer more scope – at twenty I was already a Captain and Adjutant of my regiment – and I decided to stay. Then followed a number of appointments in India, Palestine, Malaya and north-west Europe. In Malaya, during the operations against the Communist terrorists, I had an independent troop. The nature of our work meant that my Malay gunners and NCOs saw little of their families. Even when they were back at base in Kuala Lumpur no official married quarters were available. To remedy this situation I acquired a small area and some empty Nissen huts which enabled us to create our own modest village. While the operational work interested me, setting up the village gave me more satisfaction. In retrospect this tells me something about the direction I was unconsciously moving towards.

In 1956, after two years as an instructor of young officers, I attended the Staff College in Camberley which I left when I was promoted to a General Staff appointment. This ought to have been a stimulus professionally but I had begun to feel that my real interest might lie outside the services. The book that made the most impact on me at Staff College was Herbert Butterfield's *Christianity, Diplomacy and War*. I started going to church occasionally. Nothing I heard from the pulpit moved me and the services seemed to lack something, but I found a certain contentment in being in a church. I suddenly became aware that my life was very self-centred, but failed to connect this realisation with my new-found attraction for church-going. About this time, when I was thirty, a generous scheme for early retirement was announced, which would have enabled me to leave the Army then with a pension. This was the first of several occasions when I seriously considered leaving, but as I still had no definite ideas about the future, I decided to wait and take advantage of the larger pension which would become available when I reached the age of thirty-seven. For some time I had been considering the possibility of going to university as a mature student to read for a degree in philosophy while deciding my future. I had gained Oxford and Cambridge Matriculation with respectable grades, and so this was a feasible plan. But I set it aside once I had decided to carry on in the Army for a little longer.

Four years later my path to the Jesuit noviceship began to straighten out. I had spent a year on an unusual series of jobs that had taken me from the Arctic Circle down to the Sahara and back. At the end of that year, far from feeling any satisfaction, I was more than ever conscious that something was eluding me. I was growing aware that my contacts with life were really very superficial, although my life might have seemed interesting, even exciting to others. I had a great longing just to sit down and think. At the time I was spending some leave with a girlfriend's family and happened to see C. S. Lewis' *Mere Christianity* lying on a table. In an idle moment I glanced at it; to my surprise it gripped me. This moved me to take a more active interest in the church and, with baptism in view, I spoke to our chaplain, a Methodist. He introduced me to the local vicar who offered me a glass of sherry but said nothing about instruction. When I asked what I should read I was given *A History of the Church of England*. I was surprised to be offered nothing specific about faith, no catechism to give some structure to my thinking, but nevertheless I went ahead. I was baptised in May 1960 and confirmed a month later in Hereford Cathedral; I found an immediate satisfaction in going to 'Communion', but had no real idea of what I was doing. No one explained to me anything about the Eucharist but I sensed that it was somehow important to my friendship with God and the life of the church. I continued to find little meaning in Matins and Evensong. There seemed to be something missing pertaining to the origin and purpose of these services, but I assumed that I felt this way on account of my lack of experience and understanding of the church.

The following year I left for Germany to command a nuclear missile battery. It was not my choice. I had mixed feelings and had questions about the ethics of nuclear warfare. I was also reluctant to come to grips with new techniques, and had a diminished interest in command and indeed service life in general. Once again I found myself thinking about early retirement, and decided that

unless I had a radical change of heart later on, I would
seriously consider leaving at the end of the two-year tour.
After a few months I began once more to take a more
worldly view. My prospects were reasonable and even if
the business of peacetime soldiering was not very satisfying
there were exceptional opportunities for sailing, riding and
skiing which were not to be found in civilian life.

The turning-point came during my second year in Ger-
many. I had been through a difficult three months in which
I had forced myself to concentrate on even the simplest
details of work and could find no way of expressing what
I felt. It seemed as though I was carrying a lead weight,
and I was aware of being irritable and difficult to work
with. Driving home on leave that summer, I stopped off
to spend a weekend with Fr Terry Cotton, a Catholic
chaplain whom I had first met in Palestine some years
before; he was then running the Services Retreat House
in Benkhausen, north Germany. When I arrived I found
that Fr Donald Maguire, an American Jesuit, was giving a
weekend retreat for teachers. There was something natural
and peaceful about the men and women on the retreat, and
I was immediately attracted. Their manner matched the
calm atmosphere of the house which I had also noticed on
a previous visit.

I sat in on the talks given by Donald Maguire SJ, who pres-
ented everything clearly and logically. Even more significant
was his obvious zest for life. I felt I was looking in the same
direction. The weekend impressed me so much that I delayed
my return to England and listened to the talks of another
Jesuit who was giving a retreat for soldiers the following
week. For some time questions had been slowly forming in
my mind about the need for a universal church as opposed
to national churches. This had led me to read more widely.
Gradually these questions that had been half-formed for so
long were being answered: questions about the meaning of
the sacraments, the nature of the church, guiding moral
principles. Suddenly I knew I must ask for instruction in
the Roman Catholic faith. I left for England full of the
retreat-house experience but overshadowed with a kind of
fear of the strangeness of the situation. Even after I was
convinced intellectually, it took more time to overcome this

emotional barrier. As it happened, my brother and sister, each in quite different circumstances, had both been received into the Roman Catholic Church some years before, but at the time this had made no impression on me. As we were all three in different parts of the world, I had no opportunity to share my thoughts with either of them. This was a difficult time, yet strangely, I did not feel alone.

Until this point I had thought it unwise to leave the Army until I was sure of what I wanted to do. But after the retreat-house experience I began to feel that until I made the decision to go I would never find what I was looking for. While still on leave in the UK I sent in my application to retire at the earliest pensionable date, about eight months ahead, and meantime went to Norway on a temporary four-month appointment. While there I asked for instruction from the local priest in Kristiansand. The priest was a Dutch Franciscan who spoke hardly any English, but he introduced me to Wil Rondeel, a Dutch layman and a naturalised Norwegian, who proved an excellent teacher and remains a good friend today. I was received into the Catholic Church there in October 1962, during a Mass to coincide with the beginning of the Second Vatican Council. Thus I found my own 'micro' movement to God caught up in the 'macro' movement of the Catholic Church. For me, reception into the Catholic Church was a sober experience with little emotion except gratitude for those who had helped me; it just felt like coming home. I wanted to share my faith with others, although I was uncertain how this might be done – I was uneasy about evangelical enthusiasm.

I returned to Germany two days later, thinking that it would be only a matter of weeks before I went back to England and retirement. But someone was needed to start up a new training centre in the Bavarian Alps, and I was asked if I would defer retirement for a few months to plan and run this centre with German troops under my command. My first inclination was to refuse, but on reflection I thought it would be an interesting way to end twenty years of soldiering. I liked the idea of beginning my Army career at war with Germans and ending it by working with them. I agreed to stay. After a month's staff work at Army Headquarters I left for Bavaria to take up command. Later on I spent a weekend at Innsbruck where Donald Maguire SJ was doing some post-graduate work.

There was much to talk about. A month after my first communion the idea of the priesthood had occurred to me. It seemed strange, unreal, just not 'me'. I had been received into the Church only a few weeks earlier, and in any case, one of my reasons for leaving the Army was the thought of marrying and settling down like most of my friends. The idea of celibacy was difficult to accept. It took time to see celibacy as another way of loving, to realise that genuine affection is found in a loss of self – a loss in the positive sense of being taken over by the presence of so great a love that we can do no other than give ourselves uniquely to this Source of love.

While on Christmas leave I went up to the Boat Show at Earls Court. A friend, a director of one of the firms represented there, had offered me a job which sounded most attractive. But the more I thought about this, the clearer it became that what I was searching for did not lie in the direction of anything I had thought about earlier – which had ranged from work in the Probation Service or perhaps as a lay administrator in a cathedral, to buying a boat and pottering about the south coast for a year or two, supplementing my pension by painting local scenes. I still wanted to keep an open mind about the future but could not get rid of this irritating idea of the priesthood. I wanted to serve God, but I was still uncertain what form this might take.

I wrote to Fr Terry, my friend from Palestine days, setting out ten reasons for and ten reasons against becoming a priest. I didn't know it at the time, but of course this is an essential part of the discernment process. The arguments against looked so weak, I was too scared to send it. About a fortnight later I forced myself to write an elaborately casual letter hinting at vocation. Fr Terry's reply was equally casual. He said he had thought for some time that I had a vocation, and that this opinion was shared by others. I felt like a child wandering in a maze trusting to his own sense of direction, hearing a faint sound and yet unwilling to move towards it for fear that it led even deeper. I had asked God to open my mind to the truth and now that he seemed to be doing this,

I found it hard to accept. My time of prayer became more intense and earlier thoughts about the future began to fade. I was conscious of a kind of emptiness waiting to be filled.

By the spring of 1963 my work in Bavaria was completed. I took some leave in the Dolomites, and returning through Innsbruck, unexpectedly ran into Donald Maguire SJ again. He had been away for some time in the States and had only just returned that day. As he was also bound for north Germany we arranged to travel together. By the time we parted three days later I knew that whether or not I was suited to be a priest, I had to put this to the test. The Society of Jesus attracted me partly because their work seemed to lean more towards the setting up of new enterprises than to the settled life of a secular priest or a monk, but mainly because the few Jesuits I had already met were the kind of people I felt that I wanted to work with. I wrote to the British Provincial, but because of my so recent reception into the Catholic Church it appeared that I would have to wait a year at least before I could enter the noviceship. The Provincial suggested that I might consider using the interim working in a Catholic hospital or perhaps studying at Osterley, a Jesuit house for late vocations in West London. I decided on the latter.

The study year was useful in that it gave me the opportunity to brush up my Latin and find my way around the Catholic Church. I also started to paint. I was encouraged by comments on my early efforts and thought this would be useful as relaxation for the next few years when I would be a middle-aged schoolboy. I had no formal tuition in art but picked up a lot from books on painting and from just doing it. Apart from the pleasure of painting, the results look rather better today than my initial efforts and are a useful pastoral tool – they provide a talking-point. Three exhibitions have widened my pastoral contacts.

In 1964, after the year at Osterley, I began the two-year noviceship. The greatest difficulty was the age difference. For the first six months I felt as though I was in a foreign country, with a few words of the language but no idea of the grammar. Then it dawned on me that my fellow novices were saying what I said when I was eighteen. I began to understand the meaning of 'Dad, you don't understand'.

I had been eighteen in 1944. They were eighteen in 1964.
We were all listening to the same novices' conversation at
recreation time and the same Master of Novices, but my
eyes and ears were twenty years older. I was receiving on
a different wave-length.

And so to study at Heythrop, a Jesuit College, and part
of London University. Philosophy presented few problems.
Having reached the age of forty, life had made me philo-
sophical, and by the time I arrived at Heythrop in 1966 all
the lectures were given in English rather than Latin. But the
year at Osterley brushing up my Latin was not wasted. It
had put my mind into the mode of study. As for writing
essays, I found these no more difficult than the writing
up of complex military problems for staff presentations.
What was awkward was the feeling of 'being at sea', cut
off from the security of the professional competence I had
known and back at school at a time when contemporaries
were well established. But then the whole point of this
crazy idea of committing myself to a religious vocation
was that I was giving myself to God unconditionally and
could expect to be supported only by faith. At the same
time, at forty-plus I did not want to spend for ever in
studies and, reflecting on the nature of the courses, I could
see little point in doing a second year of philosophy. The
Dean was sympathetic to the suggestion that my previous
experience was a reasonable substitute for another year and
I was allowed to begin theology without delay.

When I was received into the Church my first response
had been a desire to communicate my experience of God
and something of what it means to see life through the eyes
of faith. During the noviceship I thought vaguely of doing this
through retreat work. Such thoughts were abruptly changed
in my second year of theology; the Provincial directed me
to interest myself in finance and administration with a view
to sitting alongside the Province Treasurer. Not the kind
of thinking that sets the spiritual pulses racing. I couldn't
help feeling, 'I've not joined the Society to sit in an office.'
Although I appreciated the value of sound administration, I
would have been very happy for someone else to have been
given the job. However, willingness to be available for any
kind of work ('Ignatian indifference') is what obedience is

all about, and it did not take much time in prayer to adjust to this unexpected turn of events.

In the summer of 1968, I was sent on a week's course at a well-known business school. 'Finance for the Non-financial Executive' attracted some thirty senior executives who were being groomed as high-flyers. I made friends. One of them, from IBM, introduced me to the 'Industrial Society', an organisation running many different kinds of short courses in business management. During the three years preceding ordination I did a dozen or so such courses as and when they could be fitted into my theology programme. One was a seminar for IBM's executives and another was run by the British Institute of Management. All this was unappealing at one level, but under religious obedience it is surprising how positive things can become.

The most interesting part of the courses for me was the contact with the other people attending them. After the second gin and tonic the reaction was invariably something like, 'This is the first time we've ever had a clergyman on the course, but now we find you've got arms and legs like everyone else we think it's a good idea that the church is somehow involved in what we do.' But what kind of involvement? I had met some Anglican industrial chaplains but was unconvinced by their approach which seemed more sociological than theological. I had read about the French worker-priest movement but equally did not feel there was any future in the idea of working at the same jobs as the laity.

I was as yet unclear as to exactly how I should respond as a priest. My only contact with the clergy as a layman had been largely social. Apart from some useful exercises in hearing confession and administering the sacraments, we had received little instruction on how to relate to people. I spent some time reading psychology. Then, as I neared the time of ordination, I began to feel that there might be something in the idea of being a priest among people at work as distinct from being a priest among people at home. There were precedents for this in service life and hospital chaplaincies. In 1970, shortly before ordination, I met the head of the Anglican London Industrial Mission who invited me to a seminar with the other chaplains who were covering a range of organisations based in and around London, from the docks to the east across to Heathrow Airport to the west. The Anglican chaplain there was particularly keen to have a Roman Catholic join him.

I asked the Provincial if I could have a year after ordination to find my feet as a priest before setting up a table and chair in the Treasurer's office, and if I could spend the year with the Industrial Mission exploring the idea of a priest among people at work. My request had to go through the Regional Superior for the south of England. He listened sympathetically, but I heard nothing for weeks. When I rang to ask what had happened I was told that the Province Consultors thought it best that I should work from the Jesuit community at Bristol where there was already some contact with the local Industrial Mission. A reasonable idea in itself, but I felt that the direct invitation from the London Mission offered an opening that should not be ignored. This could be Providence at work, pointing to a direction to be followed.

The Regional Superior left me free to talk to the Provincial and I rang him the same day. He told me to make my own decision; I decided to take up the offer of work with the London Mission. Our Jesuit house at Farm Street in Central London was a useful halfway between Heathrow Airport in the west and the London docks in the east; but the Superior at the time said there was no room at that particular inn. I therefore returned to Osterley in west London for my base and set about exploring the docks and Heathrow and one or two factories in between. After two months it seemed best to concentrate on the airport which had a workforce of 60,000 within its nine-mile perimeter and an ecumenical chapel at the centre: also it was conveniently close to Osterley. This looked as good a place as any to test the validity of a ministry among people at work. Six months' exploration, I thought, plus a written report on the experiment – then I would be ready to get to grips with the Treasurer's adding machine.

This plan was disrupted by an unexpected call from the Provincial's assistant to ask if I was ready to join the 1971 tertianship later in the year. Pause for thought. The tertianship is a third year of noviceship, undertaken some time after ordination and before final vows. The Instructor was the late Paul Kennedy, an outstanding spiritual guide whom I had met several times, and I knew that this might well be his last year as Tertian Instructor. The usual procedure for the tertianship was to spend the first three months making 'The Spiritual Exercises', receiving instruction, directing retreats and gaining pastoral experience away from the tertian house. Also I thought this might be an opportunity to extend the Heathrow experiment. I asked Paul if he would consider the work at Heathrow as my 'experience' and allow me to continue with it after those first three months, returning to the tertian house periodically. He agreed. My Superior at Osterley, who was very keen on the Heathrow idea, was happy to hold the fort there and ensure that the Sunday Masses were covered. Thus I joined the tertianship in September 1971 with an arrangement which surely reflects the flexibility of the Society.

With my tertianship completed in June 1972, I awaited the summons to the Treasurer's office. But events took a very different turn. On a Sunday afternoon in July that year an aircraft crashed near the Staines by-pass on the approach to Heathrow; tragically, there were no survivors. Some ten minutes after the accident I was passing the scene of the crash. Of the 118 people on board, only one little girl was still alive when I approached the site. She died as I was blessing her. I gave a general blessing to all the victims and since there was nothing more I could do immediately, went to Royal Holloway, a London University College where a large ecumenical congregation was expecting me to preach. I returned to the site of the crash as soon as I could and spent more hours with the emergency workers.

Although no stranger to death, I found something peculiarly macabre about an aircraft falling out of the sky. The gross mutilation of the bodies added to the horror of the scene. At one level I felt quite numb, at another I was strangely at peace. Time is touched by eternity at these moments. A *Daily Telegraph* reporter also happened to be passing and he took numerous photographs, including one of the child being blessed; this appeared in the press the following morning. When I finally got back to Osterley I found that the Provincial had arrived for his annual visitation and was watching the disaster on the late news. 'I think you'd better stay on at Heathrow,' he said. Over the next few days there was much pastoral work to be done there.

My experiment at Heathrow resulted in the new job of Airport Chaplain, a responsibility which was to be taken over by the Westminster Archdiocese two years later when I was asked to go as Superior to our community at Bournemouth on the south coast. By this time I had grown quite attached to the work at Heathrow and the thought of changing jobs did not appeal. Yet I was finding myself more conscious now of how we all affect each other: making decisions usually involves considering other people. No father can make a serious decision affecting the family without consulting his wife and children. One may sign an individual contract on joining an organisation but that contract has to be worked out alongside all the others in the firm. No religious can properly decide without considering the interests of their Order. A sense of family with fellow Jesuits keeps a balance. As in any family, there are many different individuals, but they are still family, and one accepts them as such – hopefully with humour.

I could think of many good reasons for staying at Heathrow, but I could also see another opportunity to put 'Ignatian indifference' into practice. After prayer and discussion, I left the decision to the Provincial. Bournemouth it was. As I had come into religious life more or less immediately after my reception into the Catholic Church, I had no parish experience – not even as a parishioner. I had to start from scratch. My predecessor had had the idea of setting up a community centre once the sale of church land for a new school had left the old one as a basis for the centre with a sufficient surplus in hand for building an extension. After some investigation I found myself in disagreement over the need for this centre on the scale proposed. However, by this time my predecessor had been appointed Provincial which made this an interesting setting for a conflict of ideas.

The conflict was dissolved on my side by his invitation for me to take over as Superior and Parish Priest at Farm Street, our largest community in London, in 1977. 'I want Farm Street to be the show-place of the Province,' he said. Among other things this meant rearranging the interior of the church to suit the liturgical changes following Vatican

II and reshaping the liturgy generally. Some changes in the community were also needed. My experience of Heathrow and its complex group of people together with the 'main-line' experience of parish work at Bournemouth proved a useful background for the work at Farm Street with its large church and international congregation. Fund-raising on a big scale was needed to finance the rebuilding of the organ, repairs to the roof and changes to the interior.

I was only ten years out of the noviceship and I found this a considerable challenge. I am most grateful for all the help and advice I received from members of the Community. In 1984, at the end of my time as Superior, I was offered a sabbatical, and was approached by a friend who said that my name had been discussed at a meeting of parents of Catholic boys at Eton College. He said that they wanted to know if I would be interested in meeting the headmaster to consider what should be done now that over ten per cent of the 1,300 boys were Catholic. How did the post of resident Chaplain appeal to me? My first reaction was that this work was not for me. Yet I was intrigued. It would be the first time since the Reformation that a Catholic priest had been invited to join the staff. I had never been and had no inclination to be involved with schools. On the other hand, 'The King's College of Our Lady of Eton besides Windsor' is rather different from any other school, being etched upon English consciousness as a national institution which, over the past six centuries, has produced numerous men to join the great and the good. Eton, moreover, seemed an appropriate area for following the Ignatian principle of influencing the influential.

I recalled a useful rule of thumb in Frank Sheed's *Society and Sanity*. 'How do you know it's the will of God?' he asks; and answers, 'It will be work you have never thought of before: it will cost you something: but in some way you will have been prepared for it by previous experience.' Well, I had never thought of anything like this before. It would certainly cost me something – I had no experience of being with boys as a group, neither had I any experience of public-school life. But in many ways my most enjoyable time in the Army had been the two years when I was an instructor of young officers;

also I liked the Etonians I had worked with over the years.

My Provincial did not take to the idea of my spending this sabbatical exploring the feasibility of the Church providing a resident Chaplain at Eton. His reasons had substance. Our Jesuit priority today is more directly with the poor and association with an élitist school like Eton would be questionable for some. There was a danger that my involvement might cut me off from the Society; and should the work become well established it might be difficult to withdraw. My own view, shared by those whom I consulted, was that a combination of work at Eton with pastoral involvement with the local parishes in the Slough Industrial Estate and surrounding areas would keep everything in balance. Our Jesuit 'fundamental *but not exclusive* option for the poor' allows flexibility in how we try to influence the influential.

After several discussions it was agreed that I should use my sabbatical to explore the Eton situation, leaving the future open. After a few months at Eton, the Provincial made his visitation and directed me to continue *pro tem*. What I had thought would be a sabbatical experiment is now in its tenth year. I have found that my own faith is fed as I try to feed the faith of the boys. It benefits all of us to have a master and a boy making suggestions for my homilies. Although I am always available to the boys, I am also involved in the neighbouring urban parishes, helping out as required. This keeps the 'catholic' or universal feel to my ministry.

Some may think of a priest's work in terms of what can be measured by attendance at Mass and the number of people knocking on his door. In fact the real value of the priest is something hidden and has more to do with the kind of person he is, rather than anything that can be quantified. Nothing much happens most of the time – I'm just around, available, trying to listen. For a priest there is no such thing as success. Success belongs to the world of sport, to banks and business; it has no place in the precincts of the sacred. The priest is sowing, never reaping, so there can be no trophies. His work is to plough the furrow, open up the earth to the seed, trusting that in God's time the harvest will come in. This is the poetry and privilege of priesthood.

The best service I can give to the Church and to Eton now,

I believe, is to try to ensure that there is continuity in the Catholic chaplaincy. In any case it is probably time for me to move on, and to start thinking about the work I could do for the Church in my forthcoming seventy-plus phase in the Society of Jesus. With the agreement of the Bishop and the headmaster therefore, I have set up the machinery for finding a successor – not necessarily another Jesuit.

What conclusions, then, after thirty years in religious life? The interplay between providence and planning weaves a mysterious pattern. 'All things work together for good for those who love God.' The conflicts and tensions are not so different from those in any walk of life. Personality clashes occur. Most of the contretemps are due to muddle rather than malice. The world is not left behind when one enters religion. The divine imperative, 'Be wise as serpents and simple as doves' (Matt 10:16) still applies. That is, wise in the ways of the world and simple in things spiritual. I value my many friendships, both with men and women. My understanding would be the poorer without them. I appreciate the values of family life even more now and am very conscious of what I have given up in following my own particular call. But I know too what I have gained: God cannot be outdone in generosity. If I had to sum up in one sentence the answer to why I stay, I would say simply, 'I *know* this is where I belong.'

Peter Knott SJ
Eton College, Windsor, UK

John English SJ

John English was born in 1924 and brought up in the prairies of Saskatchewan in western Canada. He served in the armed forces during the Second World War and gained an engineering degree before entering the Society of Jesus in 1949. After completing his training he taught briefly beforc he was appointed Master of Novices. He has been a leading pioneer in the adaptation of 'The Spiritual Exercises', making them both more relevant and more widely available, and has been influential in restoring Ignatius' method of giving 'The Exercises' to individuals on a one-to-one basis. He has also played an important role in the devclopment of spiritual communities for lay people. He is currently the Director of the Guelph Centre of Spirituality in Ontario, and the author of several books.

Chapter Seven

Spiritual Testament

I was born in 1924 and brought up on the Canadian prairies of Saskatchewan. There temperatures ranged from 105 degrees Fahrenheit in summer to minus 40 degrees in winter; we had outdoor plumbing, no electricity and a wood stove. My early years coincided with the severe economic depression of the 1930s and by modern standards we were poor. Len English, my father, had had little more than eight years' schooling, but my mother Dessa Kasenburg had been a school-teacher in a one-room school house on the prairies.

For my first ten years we lived in Dubuc, a Protestant village where my parents ran a small shop and I went to the United Church Sunday School. My brother Alex and I owned a 410 shotgun and used to go hunting on the prairies for partridge, grouse and rabbits. I remember wonderful summers on our grandparents' farm where we helped out, rode Old Bess and were generally free to wander the prairies looking for Indian arrow heads and for the nests of my grandmother's turkeys. My father was quite a sentimental man; I always found him very loving. He had high hopes for us both in the classroom and on the sports field, and we probably imbibed some of his unfulfilled ambitions. My mother had a school-teacher's penchant for correcting us, but was generally undemanding.

I was baptised as a baby, but there was little religion in either the village or my home. I can recall no mention of God for my first eleven years. Survival, school and sport were the main topics of our conversation. This changed when I was eleven and we moved to Melville, another small prairie village, where I was first conscious of being introduced to Roman Catholicism by the Oblate Fathers and Dominican Sisters who ran the local school. My mother, brother and

I were all confirmed together; I then discovered that my father's ancestry was Catholic and began to get to know the faith of my Catholic aunts, uncles and cousins.

It was at this time that my father began to drink quite heavily; he was not violent, but I was upset that he was not the ideal father. I resolved never to drink myself. During our four years at Melville I became quite pious with a special devotion to the Stations of the Cross, which I found helped me to deal with my father's drink problems. At that time I had a number of Protestant friends and seemed to be constantly defending my faith, especially my belief in the Eucharist. This must have been noticed by the Oblates at the school and they asked me to go to their junior seminary. I did not go: I felt I was too young and I had a girlfriend at the time. I was fifteen when, for financial reasons, we left Melville and returned to Dubuc where I gradually fell away from the faith. I was going through all the usual adolescent difficulties and when I was seventeen we moved yet again to Swift Current. I am sure that all this moving around in my early years affected my psychological life. I had no really permanent gang of friends and our family social life was constantly being uprooted and renewed.

I spent a year at school in Swift Current and then moved on to the University of Saskatoon to study engineering. The university was run by the Basilian Fathers who introduced me to a view of life that was both satisfying and challenging and I began to take more responsibility for my faith. It may well have been a mistake to opt for engineering – years later as a Jesuit, I realised that my basic leaning was to the humanities rather than science. But the challenge presented by engineering made it easier for me to respond to the challenge of enlistment in the Air Force in 1944. The following year I transferred to the Army, but to my chagrin when the Second World War ended in 1945, I had never left Canadian soil. Nevertheless, this period in the services was important in terms of growing up and broadening my experience, although my religious life at the time was no more than superficial.

My religious life deepened when I went to the University of British Columbia to study Forestry Engineering. While there I was influenced by an uncle and aunt, fellow students and the Redemptorists who were prominent in the university. I began to attend weekday Mass fairly regularly. I graduated in 1948 and started work as a Forestry Engineer in Winnipeg, Manitoba, where the Jesuits ran the local parish of St Ignatius. These were the first Jesuits I had met, previously I had admired their schools from afar. Now I began to work with the Jesuit priest who ran an adult sodality (spiritual fellowship) which I joined. I enjoyed helping the poor and organising a Marian Day Parade. But while I found working for the sodality exciting and fulfilling, I was experiencing failure in my occupation as an engineer. It was thus in a somewhat disconsolate and pessimistic mood that I decided to apply to enter the Jesuit novitiate in Guelph, Ontario – about a thousand miles from my prairie roots. I entered in 1949 and while I enjoyed my life in the novitiate, I can now say that I often felt that I lacked the necessary academic qualifications for Jesuit life. I saw myself as a poor, stammering, ignorant, non-Jesuit-educated individual pitched among middle-class, intelligent, eloquent, Jesuit-educated confrères.

In spite of this discouraging background, a dream that I had had when I was younger reawakened as I became incorporated into the Society. It was the dream of helping high-school students – I believed I would be good at this and felt it was significant work for anyone. As it turned out, a few years later I proved to be a proficient teacher and coach. In some ways my two-year novitiate was the happiest time of my life. The routine of prayer, reading and manual labour without the pressure of exams filled me with the desire to live out my life as a Jesuit, a desire that has remained with me always.

I was twenty-five years old when I entered the novitiate and my interior state was very confused. I had been a faithful Catholic and had found my spirituality in an adult sodality of Our Lady, yet up to that time I felt that my life had been a failure. While desiring to find my spiritual identity and vocation before God, I was filled with doubt and uncertainty. In spite of my strong attraction to the Society, I feared that I had entered the novitiate under false pretences. However, in my 'cassock retreat' I was brought up short by what Jesus said to his disciples: 'You did not choose me, no, I chose you' (Jn 15:16). These words gave me the strength to reveal all to the Master of Novices; he in turn affirmed me in my desire to live out my life as a Jesuit. The interplay between my prayer experience at that time and the Master of Novices' encouragement has remained with me on occasions of loneliness, ridicule, failure, sin and discouragement.

During my novitiate years I developed a devotion to the Sacred Heart of Jesus – a desire to put on the mind and heart of Christ; this too has remained with me. At this time also I became very attached to Ignatius and his spirituality. Ignatius was my model during formation and later became my companion. During my years of studying theology I was impressed by the theology of the Mystical Body of Christ. While I was a tertian I was given a new appreciation of Ignatius' devotion to the Trinity. These four aspects of my spiritual life – devotion to the Sacred Heart, to Ignatius and his spirituality, to the theology of the Mystical Body of Christ and to the Trinity, have continued to develop and are probably the core experience of my Jesuit identity. I have a strong conviction that I am to continue to be a Jesuit, a conviction which is enhanced by intimate fellowship with my Jesuit companions and a heightened awareness of the presence of Christ in my ministry. I consider that 'Jesuit' is part of my name.

For all this, my five years of formation in the juniorate and the study of philosophy were an extreme humiliation. My mind suggested that I was intelligent enough, but exam results were abysmal. Two years of teaching at St Paul's High School in Winnipeg during my regency restored some confidence and I therefore had some hope as I began to study theology; Elliott MacGuigan SJ was an excellent teacher and I greatly enjoyed this study. Furthermore, I was relatively successful at it and was asked to teach theology at Loyola College in Montreal after I had completed my tertianship. During this time I was also in charge of the *Jesuit Seminary Bulletin* to which I tried to bring some theological tone. The bulletins were well received, but I found then and continue to find writing a painful task.

In 1962 I went to St Beuno's in north Wales for my tertianship. There I was under the renowned Tertian Master Paul Kennedy SJ, who was a great mentor to me. This was the first time since the novitiate that I was able to realise that God truly loved me for myself and not for what I did. My appreciation of Ignatius and 'The Spiritual Exercises' deepened and my experience became the basis of much of my first book which was published some ten years later. By that time I had spent two years teaching theology at Loyola College in Montreal (1963–5) where I had to scramble to keep up to the mark with my Jesuit colleagues. I introduced Cursillo into Montreal and so had another forum of relationship with the laity. Cursillo is a method which originated in Spain whereby a priest gathers together a group of lay people for a few days and, using his theological training, explains the theological basis of their practical faith. By this method I was able to pass on the results of my serious reading of theology in a simplified but enthralling way and in so doing empower lay people to give more effective witness.

Teaching ended in 1965 when I was appointed Master of Novices at Guelph where I have lived virtually ever since, first as Novice Master, then as Director of the Guelph Centre of Spirituality and most recently as Rector of Ignatius College. My years directing the novices were very difficult. This was the immediate post-Vatican II period and everybody was scrambling to discover the meaning of formation in religious life. This was also a time of mid-life crisis for myself and also for many of my classmates who left the Society during these years. The gap they left was very painful for me. I entered into warm relationships with several families and with three or four religious women friends – possibly as compensation. Be that as it may, I continue to be grateful for these relationships with religious women who called me to ponder my living of the vowed life. For the most part they were delightful and sustained me as a Jesuit.

At Guelph my most significant work has been that of pioneering the person-to-person direction of 'The Spiritual Exercises' which has had an impact around the world. I have also been involved in beginning and promoting the Christian Life Community in Canada – a lay communal expression of Ignatian spirituality – and in the Institute for Communal Life, and have written a number of books related to this work.[1] At the present time I am the Rector of Ignatius College and am attempting to develop a deeper community sense among the four or five apostolates that emanate from this centre. I would describe this work as 'meeting Christ', the risen Christ, on the road.

My own experience spurs me on in this work, for looking

back I realise how isolated I was before I entered the Society, and how great my need was for a meaningful community; when I failed to find this my faith ceased to develop and at times seemed to disappear. Indeed, I heard little of God during my first eleven years, then between the ages of eleven and fifteen I was immersed in a milieu in which God and the Mass were all-pervasive until another move led to a year with no such support. But when I moved to university I became part of a group of young men and women who formed a lively community of faith at the Newman Club in Saskatoon.[2] After that, constant movement in the armed forces separated me once again from a faith community. With the ending of the war, yet another move brought me into touch with the Catholic Youth Organisation, an impressive faith community of which I was a part for three years. I felt totally accepted and was a member of the tennis and badminton teams. Finally, when I graduated I was fortunate in being able to find a link with the Sodality of Our Lady, a small faith community in the large city parish of Winnipeg.

Through these vicissitudes the thought of becoming a priest surfaced many times. The high spiritual element in the Sodality called me to a deeper prayer life and prepared the ground for my crisis at work as an engineer and my eventual entry into the Society. Also, around this time I had some deep religious experiences which convinced me that I should take the step of joining the Jesuits in spite of my former desire for married life. Looking back, I can discern a companionship with Jesus as I sought questions and answers, and dealt with success, sins and redemptions, suffering and joys. I recognise a kind of repetition in my life of the suffering, death and resurrection that Jesus experienced.

My present dreams have changed both on account of my Jesuit training and my experiences of ministry. My chief interest has been Ignatius' 'Spiritual Exercises', which had gradually drifted away from Ignatius' method of a one-to-one approach. Time and again during my formation I had made 'The Exercises' in a large group of anything up to forty men with a single preacher. This left little time either for personal prayer or meaningful direction. However, my six years as Master of Novices gave me a deep experiential knowledge of this instrument. It led me to design a team approach for the one-to-one directed 'Exercises', and this team method has gradually spread throughout the world. In time, I and many other Jesuits became aware that this type of retreat was somewhat limited in the dimension of social justice; we became aware that social action on its own was neither an adequate approach to Christianity nor to spiritual life. Through the Christian Life Community movement, I began devising spiritual projects for small decision-making groups such as councils or religious women or men, apostolically active groups and small communities of the laity. I believe that small Christian faith communities are the way to implement the directives of Vatican II and that they are to be a microcosm of the larger faith community.

When I consider why I stay in the Society, I know that the answer demands something more than a comparison of myself with those who have left religious life and the priesthood or with those who have undergone broken marriages. We know that God adjusts to our decisions with unconditional love and without regard to our sins and mistakes. The question also demands something more than individual consideration; it would seem to refer to the state of the Church today. Perhaps I should reword the question and ask, 'Why remain an official presence in a Church that is in some ways dysfunctional and sinful, a Church that does not seem to have much influence in our world today? What draws me to present myself as a Jesuit priest before women and men who at times consider themselves to be not only alienated from the Church, but even oppressed by it?'

As to the question of dreams, I do not think that these have been shattered as before I entered I had little opportunity for dreaming, being too much concerned with surviving. My interest was absorbed in getting a job, learning jazz piano, playing a good game of tennis or badminton, finding a wife and being paid enough to have a car, a home and a decent living. But there was always the nagging presence of priests and religious sisters living dedicated lives. Until the crisis in my work as an engineer, when I came to see that my heart was not in what I was doing, I never imagined that I could have the ability to live the life of a religious and was content with ordinary expectations. The year before I joined the Jesuits some ideals surfaced, probably on account of my experience in the Sodality at Winnipeg. Indeed, this experience may well have been the decisive factor in bringing me to the novitiate in 1949. There I admired the men who went off to the missions and performed great feats for God in India, but I knew that my lack of linguistic skills made me unsuitable. I had the more modest dream of living the novitiate rule perfectly. When I moved on to the juniorate and began to study philosophy, my main desire remained that of living the Jesuit life and passing examinations. What did stimulate my sense of purpose and awaken my dreams was my tertianship. This, made at St Beuno's under Paul Kennedy SJ, was a time of inspiration which filled me with a great desire to promote Christ's life and mission. Such desires began to be fulfilled when I was teaching theology at Loyola College in Montreal where I was able to communicate my love for Christ and his mission. Later, as Director of Novices, I was able to bring my love for 'The Exercises' to the novices and also, eventually, to many others by means of personally directing 'The Exercises'.

About this time, like many other Jesuits in their mid-forties, I was struggling to live the three vows of chastity, poverty and obedience. This was a time of emotional and intellectual confusion when my earlier ideals and personal expectations were in disarray and I felt that I was no longer living the Jesuit life as fully as I had done during my years of formation. I became discouraged, which filled me with remorse, and I felt that there was no way out of the impasse. In hindsight I am aware that this discouragement could have been caused by an idealism being shattered. But even today I do not feel that these struggles have been totally resolved, although recently I have a sense that I am living my Jesuit life more realistically. This realism would seem to affect my community responsibilities, my concern for the poor and suffering and also my prayer life. I now know myself as a sinful Jesuit and can only depend on the merciful love of God and the church as a whole.

My dreams for the ministry, however, are still with me. I am amazed to discover that the Holy Spirit is present to me and to the people with whom I share the good news of Jesus. My dreams of assisting groups to use communal discernment in decision-making and of developing small communities are becoming reality. This fills me with hope and energy for the

Church, despite my own sinfulness and despite the sinful structures of the Church. Furthermore, I see these small faith communities as the present-day instrument for re-enlivening the Church.

My life as a Jesuit is important to me. I have a conviction of my own call to celibacy. I am equally convinced of the call to other women and men who sense a unique relationship with Christ in this way and who desire to be immediately available for the service of Christ in the world. The Jesuit life is a communal experience, especially through the vow and virtue of obedience. Today Jesuits understand this obedience in terms of responsible dialogue among the whole faith community. Obedience is mediated through an appointed member of the group or congregation, who also personifies that group.

When I think about my life in the Church, I tend to separate the institutional Church from the so-called 'true' community of the faithful. Also I tend to be easily scandalised by the sinful, disordered, institutional Church and, because I represent the Church professionally, this creates a painful dichotomy within myself. I become angry with those who use their authority to place constraints upon me. I realise that I am not humble enough to deal with this communal darkness and in unguarded moments express my anger and frustration. However, my own lack of faithfulness to the ideal of Jesuit life fosters a sense of realism such as Paul expresses in Romans: 'Instead of doing the good things I want to do, I carry out the sinful things I do not want. . . . Who will rescue me from this body doomed to death? Thanks be to God through Jesus Christ our Lord!' (Rom 7:19–25). This helps me to be compassionate and patient with the unfaithful community that is the bride of Christ and to rejoice in the persons and occasions when the charity of Christ is truly expressed.

As I ponder the reasons I stay in the Society and am faced with these apparent reasons for leaving, it is a sense of the mystery or *mystique* of my relationship with the Church which provides something approaching a satisfying answer. This mystery is for me laden with meaning. It indicates the paradoxes and the mixture of ideals, good desires, and inconsistent action present within the faith community called Church. The reality of the Church is, indeed, ambiguous today; if there are sinful, disordered and unedifying elements, there are also energising, hopeful, upbuilding elements. I see the Church as a developing community that is aware of its sinfulness, yet conscious that it is called to be the discerning community of the Holy Spirit's activity in the world. It knows itself as a community at one and the same time human and divine, sinful and holy.

The Roman Catholic Church is a large social organisation of about 800,000,000 in a world population of about 5,000,000,000 people. Its government is hierarchical in the extreme. Moreover, a high proportion of its basic ministers are male, white and either European or of European extraction. Its real power is moral, based on a highly structured legal set of religious values and customs. It asserts that it represents the full truth and authentic voice of Jesus Christ and claims that it is free of error by the presence and power of the Holy Spirit operating in it, while at the same time acknowledging that other Christians have a part of the truth of Jesus Christ who is God become human. Yet from the viewpoint of many other humans beyond its authority, it is a witness of falsehood and lies. Moreover, many, even within its jurisdiction, accuse it of being male-dominated, corrupt and power-ridden. For them it is an institution which has abandoned the image of the humble Christ, who was concerned with the down-trodden and the oppressed.

At the same time, there are many holy women and men of the Catholic faith who witness love for humanity in their work in various ecumenical situations. They lovingly promote the human rights of the poor and oppressed. They have stood up for the poor and attempted to change unjust social structures. Many, including some of the Jesuit brothers, have been martyred because they sought justice, thus witnessing to the true belief in the dignity of all humans; others spend their lives in the service of the millions of the world's refugees. Many, ignoring the insidious messages conveyed by much of the media, witness to the true sense of love and peace in family life while remaining faithful to their simple devotions.

In my own ministry I am aware of the way in which the Holy Spirit is present in the lives of those I guide spiritually and in the discerning groups that I facilitate. This heightens my awareness that God has not left us alone and that Christ is present in the faith community that we call Church. Although my thoughts and activities are generally ecumenical, I continue to have a special regard for the Catholic Church of my ancestors and see her as the basic locale for me to be an instrument of God's goodness and love in our world.

My affective religious experiences have been paradoxical. They are like those of the disciples experiencing the risen Christ in their midst: 'In their joy they were disbelieving and still wondering' (Lk 24:41). So one might have contradictory experiences of security and contingency, of love and fear, of belief and questioning, of humility and fulfilment, of amazement and incredulity, of belonging and apprehension, of strength in time of weakness (cf. 2 Cor 12:9–10). There are also the affective experiences of awe, wonder, astonishment and the sense of transcendent mystery in the midst of everyday events.

The symbol of the Church as a corporate unity carries such apparent contradictions and paradoxes. Like each one of us personally, it is an example of Christ's parable of the wheat and the weeds (Mt 13:24–30). Moreover, we are each a part of the Church, we each contribute both to the grace-filled and also to the sin-filled moments of the Church's life. How can we throw the first stone? The Church is a fellowship of women and men who amaze us in their unselfishness and concern for others. But we also experience women and men who seem bent only on power and control, who act only out of self-interest and the basic disorders of corporate humanity. Yet we are bonded to this faith community. Somehow she is mother, father, brother and sister to me. I am reminded of St Peter's response to Jesus: 'Lord, who shall we go to? You have the message of eternal life.' (Jn 6:68).

Of course, all that has been said of the church applies to my relationship with the Jesuits. Each Jesuit admits that he is a sinner yet called to be a companion of Jesus as Ignatius was (G.C. 32:2,1), and the Society itself is constantly trying to transform its own sinful, disordered life to become a grace-filled expression of the Church in the world – an extension of Christ. So I sense myself as part of this paradoxical experience called Church. On the one hand I experience myself and the Church as sinful and disordered, on the other I experience myself and the Church as instruments of grace for others. This also applies to my sense of priesthood. I share in the priesthood of Christ while at the same time I am repulsed by the elements of power and control of the white male hierarchy presented under the guise of 'defending the truth'. How can I even admit to myself, let alone anyone else, that I esteem the priesthood? Obviously it has something to do with my relationship with the people of God as the extension of Christ. I guess the positive reasons and purposes of the priesthood must outweigh the negative experiences of the hierarchical Church.

Somehow my own life experience is juxtaposed with the life experience of the Church. I have strong convictions that the Church presents the basic truth of who humans are in relationship to God and the hopes of all humanity. The Church carries the truth of God's loving relationship with the universe. I see the Church as a community of all the faithful bonded together in love by the action of the Holy Spirit, regardless of worthiness or unworthiness. The Church is the bride of Christ to whom Christ is faithful even though we are unfaithful. The challenge given to Hosea to marry his adulterous wife (Hos 2:14–23), Esther's strength not to deny her people in the time of persecution (Esth 4 and 5) and Magdalene's presence at the foot of a criminal condemned by the secular courts (Jn 19:25) are powerful images that help me to deal with the apparent contradiction in the Church's life.

I have a simple faith in the 'inspired' dimension of sacred Scripture. I find that doing *lectio divina* (spiritual reading) gives me great comfort and motivation. Celebrating daily Eucharist gives me a sense of place in the faith community whether I preside and preach or whether I am present as someone else presides and I listen to one of my Jesuit brethren or a woman religious or a lay person preaching.

My main experience of finding God in all things happens within community. I find the joys and sorrows in the Jesuit community an occasion for finding God. I am also very conscious of the Spirit operating in and through me when I am present in the activity of small faith communities such as Christian Life Communities. Similarly, when I am present to individuals doing 'The Spiritual Exercises' or acting as the spiritual director of a group trying to make decisions with the mind and heart of Christ, I am conscious of being a contemplative in action.

I believe that the energy that runs our world is love. This energy is basically spiritual. It is the result of interpersonal relationships although it gets expressed materially. For this reason the centre of this energy that we call God is basically a community of persons we call the Trinity. Such love tends to diffuse itself. This we know from observation – we see the expression of this love in the beauty of the universe, our world and human persons and from the interior experience of being loved and of expressing love in totally selfless service of others. Love is relational and free. It cannot be earned. It is always a free gift. It is always given. As free beings we do not have to accept or respond, but when we do not respond we focus in on our individual selves and isolate ourselves from human relationships. Love keeps calling us and eventually we do respond first in sorrow (not guilt) and then in selfless outreach and service to others.

I believe that the basic paradigm of this interchange between the Trinity's love and human persons is expressed in the one person Jesus Christ, no doubt preceded by other human beings such as Buddha, Krishna, Hebrew Testament prophets and prophetesses, and followed by great saints such as Gandhi, Francis and Clare, Teresa and Ignatius. I believe in the *symbolic* expression of the Christian Testament. By this I mean that the actions and teachings of Jesus Christ are an expression of the way the Trinity is calling humanity and the universe into the future and their significance is never exhausted. The life, death and resurrection of Christ are the basic paradigm for us to understand our lives and to respond to Love calling us forth.

Love is always an expression of community. Jesus did not leave a manifesto or set of laws (except the law of love which is not really a law), he left a believing human community dedicated to presenting the good news of Christ's resurrection (the triumphant love of God) to all humanity. This community, known as assembly, congregation, fellowship, church, was filled with selfishness and disorder from the beginning but always recognised the mystery of the Christ among it and its need for the Holy Spirit. The basic way in which this mystery was and is expressed is in the communal experience of the faith community proclaiming its belief in the life, death and resurrection of the presence in the Eucharistic bread and wine. Coming out of the Catholic tradition, I await the day when the process of selecting 'ordained' people to focus the congregation or the community will be more in keeping with the Holy Spirit. In the meantime I believe deeply in the overarching presence and energy of the Holy Spirit, which operates in the disordered faith community and presents this mystery of Christ among us.

I have some difficulty with the existence of angels as separate entities operating in our world. I do believe that good and evil spiritual forces operate in our universe but believe that these are the sum total of the good and evil actions of human beings which get expressed in our universe and influence us significantly. Even so, there is always a need to attempt to get in touch with the Spirit of Christ, the angel par excellence.

I believe that our person continues on after death and that the Communion of Saints is with us in our constant effort to build a better world – a world of love, justice and peace. In this sense I see the Communion of Saints as the existence of the believing community beyond time and space encouraging us to persevere in good works of selfless love.

We are called to be selfless and serve each other and the whole human race. We have to face in sorrow our many disorders and the fears that lead us to a lack of response to the call of the Holy Spirit for our world. But the life of Christ and our own experience leads us to the awareness that 'where sin abounds grace does more abound' (cf. Rom 5:20).

Endnotes

1 The Institute for Communal Life, staffed by four Jesuits, works with managers of specifically Christian organisations such as school heads or parish teams and attempts to develop the use of discernment as a regular tool of management.
2 There are numerous Newman Clubs around the world. They are spiritual and intellectual associations which have been inspired by Cardinal Henry Newman's life achievement.

John English SJ
Guelph, Canada

Michael Hurley SJ

Michael Hurley SJ was born in 1923 in Ardmore, Co. Waterford, on the south coast of Ireland, and was educated at Melleray, a boarding school run by the Cistercian monks. In 1940 he joined the Society and in the course of his training studied classics at Dublin University and theology at Louvain. In 1970, after a period of teaching, he took the initiative in founding the Irish School of Ecumenics and became its Director. In 1983 he was instrumental in establishing the Columbanus Community of Reconciliation, an ecumenical and mixed community in Belfast, of which he remained a member until 1993. He is currently living in Milltown Park Community in Dublin where he is writing and directing retreats.

Chapter Eight

Triple Vocation

For me, the question 'Why stay in the Society of Jesus?' is closely related to two others: 'Why stay in the ecumenical movement?' and 'Why stay in the Catholic Church?' In my case the three questions have become largely one. I remain an ecumenist, a Jesuit and a Catholic for the same basic reason: my Christian faith has united these three vocations in such a way that each is able to make up what may at times be wanting in the others. For me the Spirit of God lives and moves in all three and is never grieved in all three together at the same time. Despite the sin and unbelief of any one or two of them, the Spirit subsists in the other(s), giving me the energy and consolation to persevere.

Every Catholic, every Jesuit therefore, is of course nowadays meant to be an ecumenist, but for all that the three vocations usually remain distinct. Not every Catholic is called to be a Jesuit. Not every Jesuit is called to have ecumenism as an occupation as well as an interest. And in my own case consciousness of the three vocations came at different times and in different circumstances. I was born a Catholic, so to speak. I became a Jesuit in my late teens. I became an ecumenist in my late thirties. It is only gradually over the years that the three have come together and forced a unity.

But where did my basic Christian faith come from? The two places where I spent my youth are both steeped in religion. Ardmore, where I was born in May 1923, is a little seaside fishing village in Co. Waterford on the south coast of Ireland which St Declan hallowed, preaching the gospel there even before St Patrick arrived. Melleray, where I was at school as a boarder from 1935 to 1940, is that bleak mountainside, also in Co. Waterford, which has been hallowed for well over a hundred years now by the worship and work of Cistercian monks. Ardmore has a round tower and other early Christian remains and a holy well. Melleray has a monastery. Both are places of devotion and pilgrimage.

My home and family were also deeply religious. It was a religion nourished by a sense of need. The twenties and thirties were difficult times in Ireland. Recovery was slow from the unsettling political and economic effects of the troubles, of the civil war which the Irish people, having achieved their independence, fought among themselves over the terms of the Treaty concluded with the British Government. My parents bought and read *The Irish Independent*; they were pro-Treaty in their sympathies. They worked hard to make a living for the four of us: my two sisters, my younger brother and myself. My mother ran a guest-house catering for summer visitors and in this work we all had to give a helping hand. My father started a small business which included selling petrol and coal and shipping the local fish catches off to the Billingsgate market in London: periwinkles in the winter, salmon in spring and lobster in summer. But as a family we remained poor, at least by modern standards. We lived frugally; summer holidays were out of the question and without a scholarship I could never have got away to secondary school.

This poverty and struggle to make ends meet coloured our religious sense and deepened our religious commitment. But our God was no mere God of the gaps on whom we depended for our temporal as well as our spiritual welfare. Our religion was much more than a comfort in difficult times; it had a deep personal quality. God was very real and near. He was a friend who also had concerns and strangely needed our help. So we shared his burdens as he shared ours. Chief among his concerns were the pagans abroad and the poor at home. These featured in our life of prayer and good works. We helped the poor out of our own poverty, like the widow in the Gospels, especially at Christmas time. We also prayed for and supported the missions. Once, I remember, a family photograph appeared in 'Colm's Corner', a feature in *The Far East,* a mission magazine which we took as well as the popular *Messenger of the Sacred Heart*.

But however personal and outgoing, our family religion in Ardmore was very traditional: it abounded in pious practices and it aimed to secure for us a safe passage and a safe entry into heaven after death. We paid visits to the Blessed Sacrament, made the Stations of the Cross, went to weekly confession and attended evening devotions – rosary and benediction – on Sundays and holy days. At home we had Mass celebrated in the house once a year and we recited the family rosary complete with trimmings every evening. In addition I served Mass regularly and during the summer I would often do so repeatedly because of the number of priests on holiday saying their private Masses on side altars. In those pre-Vatican II days each priest was bound to say his individual Mass; a joint celebration round the same altar was out of the question.

As a family we were more religiously active than the average and performed several works beyond the call of regulated obligation. These we carried out dutifully even cheerfully, not begrudgingly or resentfully, though not always too devoutly. And we were able to do so not only because of our mother's faith and fervour – our father was less devout – but also because religion in Ardmore in those days was very much a community experience and exercise, shared by the whole village, finding its supreme expression on Sunday mornings and at funerals. Life in a boarding school alongside a Cistercian monastery in the early thirties simply intensified this experience of the corporate as well as personal character of religion in an Irish village some sixty years ago.

So I grew up a pious, innocent and happy youth. At seventeen, in September 1940, I entered the Jesuit noviciate just as the London blitz was beginning. My brother followed me a few years later. Where did my Jesuit vocation come from? I had won a scholarship to boarding school and in the end I also won a scholarship to university, so despite our family circumstances, a future in some profession would have been open to me. But in fact I never thought of a secular career. My experience of organised religion and its ministers, of the Church and its priests, both at home and at school, was always positive and good. One of our curates at home became a close family friend and served as my assistant priest when I said my first Mass in 1954. One of the Cistercians in Melleray became a close personal friend. My mother's influence was also paramount but she was pushing an already open door. I had always thought of being a priest and my decision, unlike that of my brother, caused little surprise and no shock. My developing capacity for friendship and the fulfilment I was increasingly finding in friendships must have been an important factor in orientating my thoughts more towards community life in a religious order or congregation than towards the diocesan priesthood. While in Melleray I became enamoured of the Cistercian way of life and what attracted me most was its penitential aspect. Eventually, however, I was led to believe and came to accept that my particular gifts and talents seemed to indicate a calling to the Jesuits rather than the Cistercians, the intellectual apostolate being more prominent among the former than the latter.

My early years as a Jesuit followed what was then the normal pattern for those 'in formation'. Looking back now on this period, what strikes me first is how numerous we were. Twenty-one others joined with me. By the end of the noviceship in 1942 ten had left, but of the remaining twelve only one left later on. Eleven of us were eventually ordained priests and nine of us lived to celebrate our Golden Jubilees in 1990. What strikes me secondly is that all the houses in which I underwent my formation have ceased to be Jesuit institutions. The noviceship is no longer at Emo Park near Portarlington in the midlands of Ireland where I presented myself on 10 September 1940, but is now in more modest premises in the Dublin suburb of Santry. From 1942 to 1945 I lived in Rathfarnham Castle while studying classics at University College Dublin, but Rathfarnham is now sold and young Jesuits studying in Dublin live in Dundrum and Ballymun and elsewhere. From 1945 to 1948 I was in Tullabeg near Tullamore studying philosophy but Tullabeg was closed a few years ago. From Tullabeg I proceeded to Mungret College, Limerick, to teach for three years but Mungret was closed in the 1960s. From 1951 to 1955 I was in Belgium studying theology at Louvain but that house, too, has ceased to be in Jesuit hands. These facts highlight for me the very dramatic changes that have taken place in Jesuit life in my time. Since the First World War our numbers have fallen sharply but on the other hand, new forms of community have been developed and also new forms of ministry. Large establishments have given way to smaller units; there is a new appreciation of the value and importance of team work, of co-operation with others, especially lay men and women. It has been death *and* resurrection.

The happiest and probably the most formative of my early years as a Jesuit were those spent in Mungret College from 1948 to 1951. I taught Latin and Irish, supervised the study hall, assisted the headmaster, ran a Mission Society, started a social-study circle, trained my senior class to hold a debate in Latin – and managed to avoid having to take games. Opportunities seemed endless and my energies boundless. I came to life and found myself. Two experiences were particularly salutary. One morning after Mass the senior boys, instead of going to the refectory for breakfast, marched rebelliously in the opposite direction out into the grounds to a small recreation room called 'the hut' which they occupied. This hunger strike soon collapsed but months afterwards I found out that, in the eyes of some of the school authorities, I was being held responsible; that the cause allegedly was the revolutionary Marxist diet the boys were being fed in the social-study circle I ran rather than the indifferent food, as they saw it, they were being served in the refectory. I had heard nothing of this allegation until the Provincial came on visitation. I had been condemned unheard. Due process had not been observed and this interpretation of the events, if accepted by the Provincial, could have had very serious repercussions for me. Thanks however to the headmaster in whom I confided, the accusation was quashed. Indeed, the paradoxical result was that in the visitation report from the Provincial, special praise was given for the efforts being made in the school, by persons unnamed, to develop the social consciousness of the boys. And instead of postponing study of theology as a punishment, I was sent on to Louvain. But I had learnt that justice, like charity, must begin at home.

The second experience that stands out in my memory from those Mungret days is more in the area of faith than justice or politics. It emerged that one of our senior boys was not only indifferent and careless about religion but also, despite a physical presence in chapel, was already an unbeliever and an alcoholic. The boy was expelled before too long and in one of his early letters to me he wrote, 'I'm getting on fine without God.' This was 1949 and I was still a theological and spiritual innocent. The blasphemy of the phrase shocked me deeply, cut me to the quick and still haunts me. But it was a salutary if painful experience, especially for someone about to embark on a four-year course in theology. I had learnt that France was not the only European country to be a *pays de mission*.

My working life as a Jesuit falls into three parts: a decade from 1958 to 1970 teaching systematic theology at Milltown Park in Dublin to the ordinands of the Jesuit and Carmelite Orders; a decade from 1970 to 1980 also at Milltown Park but now as Director of the Irish School of Ecumenics which I had taken the initiative in founding as an interchurch institute for research and postgraduate teaching; and from 1983 to 1993 as a member of the Columbanus Community of Reconciliation which, after a sabbatical year and two years of a feasibility study, I had also taken the initiative in establishing in Belfast.

But where did this ecumenical vocation come from? I hadn't envisaged a future for myself either in theology or in ecumenism. What I had hoped for was a future in the College of Industrial Relations. And so while 'in philosophy' I made a special study of Marx's *Communist Manifesto*. While in Mungret I organised the social-study circle already mentioned. And while in Louvain I studied current developments such as Enterprise Councils and spent a good part of my first summer with the Young Christian Workers getting some experience of what life was like for a Charleroi coalminer. I spent part of the second summer in the south of France working in a steel factory. It was my superiors who, at the end of my theology, and not till then, assigned me to higher studies with a view to teaching theology.

How then did my ecumenical vocation come to develop? It all began in 1959 when the Milltown Park teaching staff decided to hold public lectures. I suggested one on the movement for Christian unity. The suggestion was accepted but, when we searched around for a speaker, we found that there seemed to be no Roman Catholic in the country who had made the subject his own. So I mugged it up myself and the lecture was so timely that I was never allowed to look back. I began to be more and more involved in interchurch relations. This ecumenical work developed side by side with my theology teaching and culminated in 1970 in two events: the commemoration in April of the centenary of the disestablishment of the Church of Ireland for which I edited a volume of essays; and the formal inauguration of the Irish School of Ecumenics in November.

But the intriguing question remains, how in 1959 did I come to suggest ecumenism as a topic for a public lecture when the Second Vatican Council had not yet taken place? Ardmore and my childhood had some part to play. We had our Church of Ireland Rector and just before the Second World War our Jewish refugees from Vienna. The Rector, a bachelor, was a tall, spare, remote figure. His congregation even in the summer was small, but still he was in no way ignored in our overwhelmingly Catholic village; I have clear memories of my father and himself chatting on the street. It was Louvain however which played the principal part in giving my life its ecumenical orientation. Protestants and Orthodox authors featured in our bibliographies. They were open to criticism of course, as were their Catholic counterparts, but their inclusion meant that they were accepted as competent to give authentic if at times erroneous interpretations of Christian faith and doctrine; their views were not *ipso facto* suspect, much less proposed for simple refutation. In addition some of my teachers, especially Père George Dejaifve SJ, were familiar with and sympathetic to the ecumenical movement. While I was in Rome doing doctoral work from 1956 to 1958, my Rector was the ecumenical pioneer, Charles Boyer SJ, whose Foyer Unitas sponsored lectures which I sometimes attended, given by such ecumenical personalities as Bishop George Bell of the Church of England. I should also note that the bishop who ordained me on 15 August 1954 was none other than Léon-Joseph Suenens who was to become one of the great influential personalities of Vatican II and who, then as Auxiliary Bishop of Malines, was fully conscious of the ecumenical tradition he was inheriting and was already aspiring to be a worthy successor to Cardinal Mercier.

Looking back now on my working years, I am amazed to see how much change was happening in my life. New horizons, new worlds were opening up for me. I was taking my first steps in interchurch relations, being introduced to Anglicanism and Methodism and Presbyterianism, and gradually coming to feel I belonged. In the second place, speaking engagements at home and abroad were multiplying and providing opportunities for travel, so I was privileged to lecture in Rome and Reykjavik, Ottawa and New Orleans, Melbourne and Minneapolis as well as in Maynooth and the Presbyterian theological college in Belfast where in 1968 I caused a storm of protest involving the college authorities in a motion of censure at General Assembly which happily was lost. In the third place there were new ventures in the beginnings of which I was very much involved: the Milltown Park public lectures, the annual Glenstal ecumenical conference, the annual Greenhills ecumenical conference, the Irish Theological Association, the Irish School of Ecumenics and the World Methodist Council–Roman Catholic Church International Commission.

In retrospect the sixties and seventies were certainly exciting. But they brought various tensions: tensions with students and tensions with colleagues – about, for instance, Bernard Lonergan SJ's theology and pluralism in theology and a preferential option for the poor; tensions with censors and superiors – about views expressed in articles intended for publication and submitted, according to Jesuit custom, for prior approval; and tensions with the Catholic hierarchy, especially in the context of the International Consultation on Mixed Marriage held in 1974 which led to strained relations with the Episcopal Commission on Ecumenism and with the Archbishop of Dublin.

By way of example, I recall an incident which took place in March 1968 at Milltown Park. One evening in the refectory after supper, the Rector made the startling public announcement that the lecture planned and announced to take place that very evening as one of the spring series had been cancelled and would not now take place; that those to act as ushers would, without further explanation, so inform those arriving for the lecture, and the lecturer himself would keep to his room. The lecturer was none other than myself. It was not that I was suddenly ill or indisposed but that higher ecclesiastical authority thought my ideas on original sin, the subject of the lecture, not altogether fit for public consumption. With hindsight I can now see how much tensions within myself – my own inadequacies and insensitivities and indiscretions – were a complicating factor in all these situations. But I managed to survive. I stayed – in the ecumenical movement, in the Society of Jesus and in the Catholic Church – because I am blessed with the precious gifts of perseverance and resilience; because at critical moments encouragement was always forthcoming from one source or another; but above all because a number of young Jesuit students, initiating an experiment in small groups living at Milltown Park in the early seventies, invited me to join them in what came to be called the Basement Community. This community turned out to be a notable success. I was an ordinary member. I did act as a sort of resident chaplain who presided at the eucharist but otherwise I had no authority. The group, however, provided me with the congenial company and support which enabled me to live happily as a Jesuit, a Catholic and an ecumenist.

When I retired as Director of the Irish School of Ecumenics in 1980, the idea was that the School, already ten years old, could begin to find its own feet without me and that after a sabbatical I would offer my services to a seminary or theo-logical college in Africa for a period of years. The sabbatical was a gloriously exhilarating experience which confirmed and renewed me in all three aspects of my vocation, not least the Jesuit one, and set me off in an altogether unexpected direction. I was breaking fresh ground both geographically and ecumenically as I travelled in Greece and the Holy Land, in Africa and India and got into China on what was the end of the medieval silk route at Xian and further on to Peking.

This was my first real experience of the other world reli-gions and it left me with challenging, indeed disturbing questions, especially about Islam which shouldn't, I couldn't help feeling, have been able to conquer Christianity in places like Egypt and to forestall it in places like north India. But it was my Jesuit vocation which, I think, benefited most from the sabbatical. A Jesuit, I discovered in a new way during the year, is someone who is fortunate enough to have a home from home all over the world. He belongs to a far-flung company of men who, like the rest, are sinners but who, at their best, are generous, bold and imaginative in their devotion to and service of Christ and the gospel. I never before felt so grateful for, so proud indeed, of my Jesuit vocation as when I attended Mass at the Tan Tang, the seventeenth-century Jesuit church in Peking, and prayed at the tombs of the pioneering Jesuits

Ricci, Verbiest and Schall, and visited Agra and Fatehpur Sikri where in the sixteenth century the Mogul Emperor, Akbar, had Jesuits at his court; or when I stayed with Jesuits in such a variety of places as the island of Syros, Addis Ababa, Varanasi, Kathmandu and of course Zambia and Hong Kong where Irish Jesuits, my own brother included, have laboured so devotedly this century.

The main result of my sabbatical (1980–1) was the Columbanus Community of Reconciliation. Instead of teaching theology in Port Harcourt or Nairobi or some place else in Africa as envisaged originally, I have since my return been helping to get an interchurch residential community off the ground in Belfast, a city notorious for its sectarianism. The idea came into my head in the middle of a thirty-day retreat which I was doing in the little Indian village of Sitagarha near Hazaribagh, in north-east India. It had been in my mind in 1969 as is clear from the last chapter and last page of *Irish Anglicanism* but it had disappeared from my consciousness during the seventies and emerged as a completely new suggestion in February 1981. An attempt however by a religious to start some sort of an interdenominational residential community can only seem entirely logical if one of the basic insights of the ecumenical movement is that the churches should do everything together as far as conscience permits. For an ecumenist, too, it could only seem entirely logical to feel called to undertake such an initiative in a place where the scandal of Christian disunity is particularly grave. After the retreat, therefore, the idea grew on me and seemed good to some, though not to all, of the Jesuit friends whom I consulted. In particular it commended itself to my Provincial Superior who on my return home in the summer of 1981 suggested that I carry out a feasibility study.

The moment could hardly have been more inauspicious. The feasibility study happened, unfortunately, to coincide with the most difficult and tense years in the whole tempestuous history of the Jesuits. Relations between the Society of Jesus and the papacy reached an all-time low in 1981 when the Pope intervened in the normal procedures of Jesuit government and nominated a delegate of his own to govern the Society. Reactions varied: there was much support and sympathy but also much embarrassment and confusion as well as indignation and anger among Jesuits. Happily, before too long communication and confidence were restored and the storm blew over. But while it lasted it was hardly the most propitious moment for Jesuits to get involved in, much less take a leading part in, a new and ecumenical initiative. But despite the general nervousness of the times, my superiors, so far from discouraging me or in an excess of caution suggesting that I postpone the venture for the moment, gave me their full support insisting only that I proceed with the utmost care and correctness.

So it was that early on I sought and secured interviews with Cardinal O'Fiaich, with two members of the Episcopal Commission on Ecumenism (Bishop Cahal Daly, then in Longford, and the late Bishop Kevin McNamara, then in Kerry), with the President of the Vatican Unity Secretariat (as it was then called), Cardinal Willebrands and with the Vice-President, Bishop Torrella. The reaction of all five was quite positive though understandably guarded and cautionary on the question of eucharistic sharing. The reaction of the other churches was also positive and in due course the Columbanus Community was formally inaugurated at 683 Antrim Road in Belfast on 23 November 1983. This was the feast day of St Columbanus, the younger contemporary of Columba of Derry and Iona, who has been called Ireland's first European because he went from Bangor, Co. Down, to establish communities at Luxeuil in France and at Bobbio in Italy. He died in 615.

When I retired as Director of the School of Ecumenics in 1980, the angel of the church in Milltown Park might well have addressed me in the words used of old by his colleague in Ephesus: 'I know, too, that you have patience, and have suffered for my name without growing tired. Nevertheless I have this complaint to make; you have less love now than you used to.' (Rev 2:3–4). He might even have made his own the words of his Sardis colleague: 'I know all about you: how you are reputed to be alive and yet are dead. Wake up; revive what little you have left: it is dying fast. So far I have failed to notice anything in the way you live that my God could possibly call perfect.' (Rev 3:2) It is easier perhaps in the Columbanus Community to hear and obey what the Spirit is saying. By contrast with the School of Ecumenics, the task here is more spiritual than intellectual, though of course the Community has its intellectual, as the School has its spiritual, dimension.

Prayer – and prayer together – is an essential part of the Columbanus Way. We meet for prayer morning and evening – and at midday if we happen to be at home. We also celebrate the eucharist together every day except Sundays, though attendance is optional and we refrain at present from eucharistic sharing. On the strength of this regime of common prayer we live together as Catholics and Protestants a life of unity, simplicity and peace. In this way we offer a practical challenge to the sectarianism, injustice and violence prevalent all around us. We also run a small centre in our own premises where lectures and quiet days of prayer are held and appropriate courses of unity, peace and justice are given, and we help outside to service the work of other agencies. But the whole ecumenical spirituality which in a variety of ways we try to practise is solidly based on a life of prayer within the Community. It is of course also dependent on encouragement from without; happily right from the beginning this has been forthcoming in a measure which more than counterbalances the discouragement arising from the persistent nature of the conflict.

As I write I am preparing to retire from the Columbanus Community in order to enable it to find its own feet without me. As I do so honours are being showered on me. I have been invested with the Coventry Cross of Nails by the Cathedral Provost. I have received an honorary LL.D from the Queen's University of Belfast. A book of essays has been published in my honour and the book's launch was attended by all the Irish church leaders. But honours are onerous and there is evangelical truth in what Shakespeare says about honour being 'a burden too heavy for a man that hopes for heaven'. In addition I should find it difficult to maintain that success is a Christian concept or reality. According to the 'First Principle and Foundation' of 'The Spiritual Exercises', I cannot prefer failure to success or vice versa. But according to the 'Third Kind of Humility', must I not desire and choose, must I not prefer failure with Christ on the cross rather than success 'provided equal or greater praise and service be given to the Divine Majesty'?

So I keep reminding myself how fragile and vulnerable the Irish School of Ecumenics and the Columbanus Community of Reconciliation both are, how precarious their existence, and how my generation of Jesuits has failed to attract vocations in the First World and has failed everywhere to integrate work for justice and work for Christian unity. I also ask myself whether I haven't seriously compromised the gospel and my triple vocation. Have I perhaps acquiesced in the ecumenical status quo rather than struggle to change it? Have I accepted pietism, the besetting weakness of Northern Ireland Christianity, rather than trying to reform it? Being a Christian must surely include acknowledging my sinfulness and having my life and work signed with the sign of the cross. And being, staying a Christian is the whole basis of my vocation as an ecumenist, a Jesuit and a Catholic.

Michael Hurley SJ
Dublin, Ireland

Peter Steele SJ

Peter Steele was born in Perth, Western Australia in 1939 and was educated by the Christian Brothers. In 1957 he joined the Society of Jesus. He both studied and has taught at Melbourne University, where he currently has a personal Chair. From 1985 to 1990 he served as Provincial of the Society of Jesus in Australia. He is a poet and has published two books of poetry, several books on literary criticism and many articles on both literature and spirituality.

Chapter Nine

Unambiguous Commitment

I had never met a Jesuit until a couple of years before I finished my secondary schooling. I was born a week before the beginning of the Second World War, and grew up in Perth, Western Australia, the eldest in a family of three boys. My father had emigrated to Australia from England at the age of nineteen, with his widowed mother and his sister and two brothers. He was a quick-witted and resolute man, deprived by family circumstances of the opportunity to complete his own secondary schooling. All his life, even though he held a number of positions of responsibility, he probably suffered from a sense of denied opportunity. Brought up as an Anglican, he became a Catholic when he married my mother, who is an Australian of mixed English and Irish stock.

I was educated within the Catholic primary and secondary school system, first by the Sisters of Mercy and then by the Christian Brothers. Montaigne said that he had a bad memory, which may have been an affectation; I really do have a bad memory with the result that isolated images swim back to me in recollection, but give little sense of the run or the feel of whole days, let alone whole years.

A committed Catholicism was central to our household. There was nothing fanatical about this, but Catholicism provided the ethos, in a matter-of-fact way. When my father became a Catholic he did so as a matter of principle rather than because he was marrying a Catholic, and he lived out the implications of that decision, as he saw them, until his death a few years ago. My mother was the youngest child of a large family which had made its way on the land and then moved into the city. While she had been brought up with and maintains the pieties and demands often associated with the Irish Catholic tradition, she must have been her own woman from an early age, and her identity included religious commitment as the most important thing in life.

My earliest memory is of seeing my brother, three years younger than myself, on the day of his birth; my next earliest of seeing my father doing some household mending just before going off to New Guinea to fight during the Second World War. Like millions of men throughout the centuries who came back from the wars, he was for years a spent man physically and, to a degree, emotionally. Unlike my father's family in earlier years, we were not in penury. But things had to be done without – there was no car, no telephone and little that we could identify as a luxury. To put all three boys through church schooling, which was insisted upon as a duty wherever it was possible, was demanding for people of limited means. But it was as high on my parents' list of priorities as regular attendance at Mass and frequent recitation of the rosary. My father was the least ostentatious of men, religiously speaking, but an abiding memory is the moment when he, my mother and myself entered St Peter's in Rome for the first time and he made briskly for an appropriate spot to begin the rosary. This was both a piece of cultural continuity and, by then, a personal salute.

It was accepted when I was well short of my teens that I was going to be a priest. I cannot reconstruct the process by which this came about initially, and although it might matter to a therapist, it doesn't matter to me. The notion was encouraged, though never enforced, by my parents – and I suppose that I was pious, though I would not bet on that. Years ago, when I told my mother that I remembered myself as a taciturn child, she burst into incredulous laughter – as would all my friends today.

Pious or not, I was certainly bookish. Few books were at home, but the school library was well stocked, and for years my Christmas present was a subscription to the Central Catholic Library which I loved. That respectable form of gluttony, gorging on the printed word, took hold on me very early. Autobiography, biography, travel writing and history were particular favourites. And I was constantly interested in the Christian or Catholic vision of life of which

I had first-hand experience and which I wanted to make as widely available as possible.

I may have preened myself when, having read everything I could find by G. K. Chesterton, I moved on to Thomas Aquinas. But there was little affectation about it all, and books read in those formative years continue to nourish and challenge me today. At about the same time, I began to come across the initials 'SJ' at the foot of articles or on the title pages of books. This started with the pamphlets of Daniel Lord SJ, but I also came across the writings of other American Jesuits as well as those of English and Irish ones. I was struck by a sense that the Jesuits knew what they were about, and that there was always an edge to their minds. They seemed to be informed, intelligent and dedicated, and gave the impression of wanting to be useful on a generous scale. With or without good reason, I thought of myself in similar terms. For years I had been sharing the academic honours of school with another boy and I had had some experience of other forms of leadership which never, alas, included anything to do with sport – on a cricket or football field I was like the Ninevites in the Book of Jonah, who could not tell their left hand from their right. But it was not until one of the Christian Brothers who knew that I was bent on priesthood asked me whether I had ever considered the Jesuits that my interest quickened.

Although there was a Jesuit school in Perth, I had never had anything to do with it. Ignorance fostered my assumption that it was snobbish: it was, in any case, on the 'right' side of the city, which meant that it was on the wrong side as far as I was concerned. The Jesuits to whom I was introduced were, however, men whom I could like as well as admire, and bit by bit it was settled that I should join the Jesuit novitiate in Melbourne. From Perth to Melbourne took two days and three nights by train, and the exodus itself was a rite of passage: I was leaving not only family and friends, but my known world. My mother, an indomitable traveller, came along for the ride. I left Perth sunburned to arrive in a drizzled-upon Melbourne. I was seventeen then, and for all but three of the next thirty-seven years I have been based in Melbourne.

As I look back now at the thin, tense young man who

made his way into the hulking ecclesiastical building on the outskirts of Melbourne in early 1957, I find various things to dislike – the self-absorption, the compound of timidity and provincial cockiness, the proclivity of seeing the mind as a blade rather than as a resource for the fostering of joy in life – but he and I are identical in at least one respect: he was convinced that he was called by God to unambiguous commitment, and so I remain. Then as now I thought of myself as a summoned person in a summoned world, and the way to live this out seemed to lie in becoming a priest.

The long haul of Jesuit formation reflects in many ways the longer haul of life-formation. I did not know this when I began the Jesuit training, whose successive stages can easily dispose one to believe that one will, one day, emerge from a series of earlier drafts as the definitive version. Yet even then I sensed that I, and the world at large called for celebration: and I thought – and still think – that priests exist in order to enable that celebration to take place.

Most celebrations involve some kind of sacrifice, and the Ignatian stress on the need for self transformation made sense in that context. The need, of course, is not peculiar to the Ignatian spiritual tradition, since it lies at the heart of the gospel. I believe that priesthood implies singing the praises of creation and the Creator, as well as lamenting what we have made of the past and what we are making of the present. It also has a role in enabling transformation to come about. All this takes place ritually and momentously through the Mass and the other sacraments, and it is there that I find the most significant meaning in my own life and in the life of the world. A Eucharist which failed to look towards the transformation of the world and of the lives of the participants would be a contradiction in terms.

Whether I am celebrating Mass with a handful of Christians or on a more sizeable public occasion, I am always conscious that things are going to have to change, and I have always thought of education as being, in the widest sense, an agent of change. It is humiliating to see how slight change for good appears to be. In the conclusion to Rilke's poem 'Archaic Torso of Apollo', he says simply, 'You must change your life.' The Ignatian preoccupation with daily change is of a piece with that.

The dozen or so of us who entered the novitiate together would not have put things in that way. But we were on the road, and our Novice-master, Ned Riordan SJ, a veteran ascetic who coupled divine wisdom with human shrewdness, was a good hand at steering us in the right direction. Most of that group are still Jesuits – something we would all have taken for granted when we were novices, but which was to become statistically improbable as other events unfolded.

For the most part we were an intellectually gifted bunch, and when we took our vows and began to study philosophy, we had one uncommonly challenging teacher in the meta-physician Pat McEvoy SJ, who stretched us to the limit. Lectures were always in Latin in those days which was an affliction for some of us; for a few others it was a way of keying the heart more decisively into a God engaged with his world. McEvoy kept stringently to philosophical rather than theological matters, but his portrayal of the dynamic of the human spirit being met by the Divine Spirit stressed the 'ever-greater' God who is mysteriously *en rapport* with his creatures. Although I do not have the philosophical mind, I read virtually nothing but philosophy and spirituality over a period of three years. If this was a demanding pleasure, it was also at that time the available way of pursuing Christ on my pilgrimage.

In the early sixties my year went to the University, and the bow-wave of Vatican II hit Australia. The University of Melbourne, in which I am still a teacher, was secular in every way. Catholics were in a minority, and were there on sufferance. The highly-motivated, black-clad Jesuits were five years older than most in their academic group and, leading relatively simple lives, had the irritating habit of cleaning up the honours in the comparatively narrow range of disciplines in which they contended. We came and went by minibus; a solemn young Jesuit, a little older than myself assured me that our policy should be to attend classes, use the library and otherwise have as little as possible to do with the University. If the SAS are known to some as 'The Hooligans', I can only guess what our lot may have been called behind our backs!

All this began for me in 1962. I regard it as one of the discernibly providential developments in my life that

I should so soon have become involved in the Newman
Society, otherwise known as the Apostolate, an essentially
lay Catholic movement within the University. Fragments of
the history of this venture have been written by its supporters
and its detractors as well as by one or two objective observ-
ers. Under the charismatic leadership of Vincent Buckley it
provided me with a dynamic interchange between the secular
and the sacred. Buckley was a poet and critic of distinction,
and a teacher of magisterial flair. In his company, and in that
of those who were likeminded, I developed a stronger and
more explicit sense of the correlation between the human
and the divine. Like various other people, with a degree
of foresight I had come to take for granted some of the
emphases which were to be drawn when the Vatican Council
promulgated the document *Gaudium et Spes* on 'The Church
in the Modern World' in December 1965. The fact that I saw
this coming says more about the social ambience in which I
was moving than about any degree of theological alertness
I might have possessed.

If there is an element of the unpredictable about individ-
uals joining the Society, there is equally an unpredictable
element about their staying. The sixties, in Australia as
elsewhere, saw a revolving door of entries and exits, in
both cases sometimes well considered. For myself, it was
in large measure due to the lay Catholic Newman Society
that my sense of commitment to God as a member of a
religious order was confirmed in learning to value things
precious to my Catholic friends at the University, I could
also see my Jesuit calling more clearly. And as I began
increasingly to relish the life of the mind, my sense of being
both God-haunted and a God-hunter strengthened.

Throughout my life I have been moved tellingly by many
books. Ida Friederike Gorres speaks, in her *Broken Lights,*
of what she calls 'books providence' – coming across the
right book at the right time. Many a human being has been
decisively and disastrously swaddled in paper all through life,
but I do not doubt that for me all that black-lettering has
been, on the whole, luminous. Whether I was reading Donne
or Montaigne, Barth or Weber, I was receiving a transfusion
of the spirit. The ancient monastic practice of *lectio divina* is
precious indeed. There is also such a thing as *lectio humana*

– a steeping of the soul in another soul, mediated by means of words in all their fragility and vitality. At school I had been a scribbler, in the seminary a jotter; as a Jesuit at the University, I became a writer. Those last ten words resume, in practice, the answer to the original question 'Why stay?' Everything that broadened my horizon intensified my sense of how, essentially, I should live under that horizon. A junior in the company of teachers, I was trying to find out where the skiff of the word would take me.

John Updike says, 'The artist's personality has an awkward ambivalence: he is a cave dweller who yet hopes to be pursued into his cave.' This mingling of the instinct for privacy and the hope to be made public applies to two other groups apart from writers – teachers of a certain sort, and 'active' religious among whom are Jesuits. Early on my superiors decided that I should be a teacher at the University, and so I have been since the mid-sixties. In prizing highly the teaching vocation, the Society of Jesus has continued a form of Christian humanism. The question 'Why remain a Jesuit teacher?' elicits the answer, so far as I am concerned, 'Because that is where the drama of a graced and grace-resisting world is best played out.' I have no doubt that the exercise is worth the effort.

For Ignatius, every mission unfolded out of mysticism: it was the God in the heart who sent one out to meet God in the world. If the Jesuit reroots himself daily in the ground of his being, he may hope to have fruit to offer to the world at large. Often, of course, it seems not to turn out that way. George Herbert, afflicted by a sense of futility, says in one of his poems, 'Oh that I was an orange tree, That busy plant.' Mere busyness can jeopardise deep fruitfulness – perhaps the characteristic Jesuit blunder. But when one is running true, life makes room for a drama of the spirit every day.

That, I take it, is why Ignatius places such extraordinary stress on the value of repeated examinations of one's 'alertness'. He assumes, on the basis of personal experience, that divinity is accepted or rejected in the midst of everything that happens – the shower taken, the path walked to work, the casual conversations, the reading and writing and teaching, the meals – in short, the sum total of activity. A friend who said that a priest is in reality a person who is becoming a priest was not being whimsical; he was offering an evolutionary, a developmental model of how one stays the course. In one sense, this is a public affair; in another, it is entirely personal and incommunicable. Auden said that while there is a game called Cops and Robbers, there is no game called Saints and Sinners.

By the mid-sixties I was writing poetry, helped both by past poets and contemporary mentors. I wrote too little poetry and too much prose, as I still do, but one reason for the prosing was to try to wed secular to sacred for my own devotional purposes and in order to provide some kind of model for my Jesuit confrères to adopt or improve upon. For me to ply the secular craft of writing is itself a form of readopting the religious vocation.

Through the sixties and seventies I spent countless hours listening to young Jesuits who were making up their minds whether to stay or to go. Most of them went, and were right to do so, and most of those who stayed were the better for their doubts. I do not make light of the institution's capacity for social insensitivity or for outright repression when I say that hardly any of those I knew who left did so as a result of inappropriate demands made by the Society. True, there were cloth-headed regulations, and there were men who were themselves falling apart who yet tried to put others together; pain was caused and damage was done. But when all the chips were down, the men who stayed were those for whom religious life was a humane and divine imperative. The others left. In a wounded world, that is about the best one can hope for.

As far as the Society of Jesus is concerned, the sixties, seventies and eighties were notoriously exacting. Partly in response to things happening in the Church as a whole and in the wider world, and partly as a consequence of internal events, the Society tried to reappraise and transform itself. Accounts of this process range from seamless self-congratulation to indefatigable malice – the latter, of course, making for larger royalties. For better or worse, I was neither shocked nor shaken by most of this any more than by sundry things happening in the church at large.

Had I been a professional theologian, things might have been different. It cannot be pleasant for a grown person of ecclesial commitment and intellectual passion to be treated as a naughty child by some nameless scrivener who has managed to have his letter signed by one of the mighty. Knowing my temperament, had I been in such a predicament I would probably have slumped into depression, thus giving yet another hostage to fortune. In the early sixties one of my superiors said to me, 'You should study literature and concentrate on poetry. Over in Rome they think that all poets are mad and they leave them alone.' There were probably better reasons for leaving me alone, but it is an interesting thesis and marginally more genial than the comment of one of my contemporaries made at about the same time: 'If they ever work out what you're talking about, they'll either make you Provincial or kick you out.' They eventually made me Provincial, while that contemporary is now an Anglican priest.

In my early thirties I was appointed as one of the Provincial's official advisers, and shortly after that as superior of a houseful of younger Jesuits who were studying at the University. Not for the first time, I was reminded of the saying that life is a comedy for those who think and a tragedy for those who feel; most of us think a bit and feel a bit, and so our responses are varied. It was a strenuous time for me. I was teaching full-time, writing a doctoral dissertation, acting as adviser to the Provincial, and doing various odd jobs around the Province. To care adequately for several dozen gifted young men, and a few of their elders, in those circumstances was difficult and perhaps impossible. I believed that they had more motivation and greater powers of self analysis than could in fact have been the case. These were also the years in which the 'generation of '68' was having a crucial influence in a variety of ways. I needed all the help I could get from my conviction that the life of groups, like that of individuals, evolves. 'When two or three are gathered together, that is about enough,' wrote Les Murray.

With those tasks completed, I continued to teach in the University until 1984, when I was on sabbatical leave in Chicago, writing some lectures to be given at Oxford at the end of the year, and doing no harm to anybody. Two things happened simultaneously. I was invited to fly back to Australia to be interviewed, in a short list of two, for the Chair of English at Melbourne, and I was informed that I had been appointed Provincial of Australia and New Zealand. A telephone call disposed of the first possibility, and doing something I hadn't done for a while, namely making the Stations of the Cross, got me in order for the second. Vexed friends rang me to deplore, courteously, this decision of the Society of Jesus, and looking back I can see the force of their argument; without self-preening, I can see that there were real public losses as a result of this outcome. But so it goes; and whether or not the University's loss was the Jesuits' gain, I myself gained a great deal from the subsequent six years.

The work of a Provincial may be summed up as 'listening to the other side' and 'doing something about it'. A Provincial spends the bulk of his time listening to other people, whether in absolutely confidential situations, or in broader meetings, and whether he likes it or not, other people set a large part of the emotional, intellectual and spiritual agenda. The Irish joke that when a man becomes a bishop he will never again eat a bad meal or be told the truth is exactly reversed when it comes to being a Provincial: he eats, on his peregrinations, a lot of very strange food, and he is told more truth than he can easily deal with. Peregrinations they are, at least hereabouts: my predecessor told me that he had travelled half a million air-miles in his six years' stint, and I would have done all of that within Australia and beyond.

It is no secret that the tasks of this role can burn a person out. While I was still in office, a visiting American Jesuit ex-Provincial told a group in Australia that in North America about forty per cent of former religious major superiors either left their Orders or permanently marginalised themselves. Although not inclined to do either of these things, I found this completely understandable. Office is lonely, the served often do not understand or cherish their servants, expectations are pitched high even while energies may be low, the Ignatian ethos of shooting for the stars can turn a weapon upon the vehicle that fails to lift off. In short, being a Provincial is a messy business, but as I often said, I enjoyed it (and that was frequently true). When it was over, I described it as the best thing that has happened to me.

Half way through the six-year hitch, following good advice,

I took a couple of months off and went back to a favourite Jesuit community in Chicago. Over a drink there, friends asked me what was the hardest thing about the job. 'Dealing with the crazies', I said. I had in mind not only the transient neuroses or occasional lunacies to be found in any sizeable body of human beings, but also the reverberations set off by people with specific difficulties and by those of us who despite our fragility attempt to help them.

But for all that, when I contemplate the breathtaking beauty which the human race has accomplished, and the vileness which we have perpetrated, defacing thereby the image of God, the inadequacies of the contemporary Society of Jesus or of the Catholic Church do not seem to me to be unduly significant. No doubt we should all be better, but who can cast the first stone?

My 'vision' for the Church and for that of the Society of Jesus is to be found in the documents of Vatican II, and in the documents of the last three General Congregations of the Society. I have a motley array of heroes when it comes to humane, theological and spiritual insight. These include Chesterton, Hannah Arendt, Karl Barth, Karl Rahner, Hans Urs Von Balthasar, Dan Berrigan, Bruno Bettelheim and Thomas Merton. And I have a ragged choir of poets, ancient and modern, singing in my head much of the time, among them Donne, Browning, Whitman, Dickinson, Yeats and Heaney. But precisely because I have earned my bread by dealing in the word for most of my adult life, it seems to me to be a form of superstition to be affronted by the hiatus between word and deed.

I try to be engaged with the present predicament of 'my' people, but I think that it behoves all of us to think in terms of the next hundred or thousand years, and occasionally the next million. Emmanuel Mounier wrote once, 'For all we know, we may be first-generation Christians.' We have no way whatever of knowing whether that conjecture will be vindicated, but we are likely to be calmer, more resolute and also more hope-driven if we think of ourselves in such terms.

Why do I stay? Given what has happened, why not? In the following lines the poet Updike speaks to me of more than writing when he says, 'To become less and transmit more, to replenish energy with wisdom – some such hope, at this more than mid-point of my life, is the reason why I write.' It is more than enough reason why I remain a Jesuit. It is more than enough reason to live.

Peter Steele SJ
Melbourne, Australia

Glossary

Apostolate: The work a person does in fulfilment of her/his calling. E.g., giving retreats, teaching, writing, working in a parish.

Bull (Papal Bull): A papal authorisation. E.g., the Edict authorising and approving the setting up of the Society of Jesus.

Cassock Retreat: In the early weeks of the novitiate (see below), the novice makes a short retreat at the end of which it used to be the custom to receive a cassock (or gown) which he then customarily wore during the novitiate.

Charism: Gift of the Holy Spirit. We can speak of the charism of a particular person or group, meaning how that person or group is particularly gifted. E.g., the charism of St Francis of Assisi was his love of poverty; the charism of the Society of Jesus is 'to find God in all things'. The charism points to the character of the person or group.

General Congregation: The highest legislative body in the Society of Jesus under the Pope. Even the Superior General is bound by its decrees; his ordinary government consists largely in administering them. At this present time the Society is preparing for its thirty-fourth General Congregation.

Grades: Ignatius established the following grades (or classes) of members: the *professed* are priests who make solemn vows of poverty, chastity and obedience plus an additional vow of obedience to the Pope with regard to mission; the *spiritual coadjutors* are priests who make final vows of poverty, chastity and obedience; and the *temporal coadjutors* (Brothers) who are laymen and who make similar final vows. Those who have made final vows are formed Jesuits; those 'in formation' make up a fourth grade, the *scholastics* and *brothers* who, at the end of their novitiate, make simple but perpetual vows of poverty, chastity and obedience and promise to become full members after they have completed their training.

Lectio Divina: Spiritual reading, often obligatory for members of religious communities.

Novitiate: A man on entering the Society spends his first two years doing his novitiate. It is a period of time when he seeks to confirm his vocation to the Society and the Society considers whether or not he is a likely recruit. During the novitiate he will make the full 'Exercises', study the history of the Society and reflect upon its nature, and engage in a variety of apostolic activities.

The Hebrew Bible: Consists of the Old Testament without the Apocrypha.

The National Project of Religious Education was initiated in 1985 under the auspices of the Bishops' Conference of England and Wales. It was envisaged that an agreed programme of religious education would be produced beginning with preschool children and continuing into adulthood.

Novice: A man making his novitiate.

Plan of Studies (Ratio Studiorum): The definitive Plan of Studies was published by Father General Aquaviva in 1599; it governed practice in Jesuit schools till the suppression in 1773. In its complete form it gives directives for an entire Jesuit University. The *Ratio* is, however, more a treatment of curricular organisation and pedagogical procedure than of educational theory. After the restoration of the Society, the General, Father Jan Roothan, directed the revision of the *Ratio*, but this revision was never approved by a General Congregation. Nevertheless, the *Ratio* continued to influence the direction of Jesuit studies.

Prefect of Studies: Jesuit in charge of a Jesuit school – equivalent to headmaster.

Reductions (Paraguay): The Reductions were communities

of Christians first established by Jesuits working in Paraguay in 1610. By 1767, the year of their expulsion, the Jesuits had fifty-seven Reductions with a population of 113,716. Each Reduction, besides being a religious community, was also a self-contained socioeconomic unit. The name is derived from the Latin *reducir* ('brought back') because the indigenous people had been brought back from the wilds and forests by the preaching of the missionaries to live in organised communities under Christian laws.

Retreat: A time of retreat from one's normal everyday occupations for the purpose of prayer and reflection. Making 'The Spiritual Exercises' of Ignatius requires some degree of seclusion and silence by a person involved in the full Exercises of Thirty Days or some modified version of them. A Jesuit will generally do an eight-day retreat each year.

Retreatant: A person making a retreat.

Residency: House. Formed (see grades) Jesuits who had completed their studies and were engaged in a variety of different apostolic works were to live in houses exclusively supported by alms.

Scholastic: See under grades.

Society: Always stands for Society of Jesus.

Spiritual Life: A life led according to certain norms of behaviour. For the Christian, it would be a life led according to the spirit of the gospel.

Spiritual Direction: Spiritual Direction is a life-long process upon which a person embarks when she/he engages in conversation with a Spiritual Director about her/his spiritual life. It is a relationship of friendship and care (rather than 'direction') in which a person with the help of a 'director' seeks to discover what is the will God for her/him.

Spiritual Director: A person skilled in giving spiritual direction. A 'director' does not so much 'direct' but helps the person reflect and piece together the relevant and important experiences of her/his life.

Discernment: Discernment is the process by which a person seeks to discover what is the will of God for her/him.

Spiritual Exercises: 'The Spiritual Exercises' of St Ignatius (to give them their full title) were written as a result of his own conversion experience. Ignatius sets out with great precision the movements or stages in his conversion in such a way that a person following 'The Exercises' is enabled and moved to reflect upon her/his own experiences in a way which will lead her/him towards conversion and a closer following of Christ. The full 'Exercises' are divided into four stages (or Weeks) and generally take about thirty days to do.

Tertian Year (tertianship): The tertianship is the final period of formation. It takes place some years after ordination to the priesthood or after ten years of life in the Society for Brothers. It consists in making again the full 'Exercises' and studying the Constitutions of the Society of Jesus. It may also include involvement in a variety of apostolic experiences.

Tonsured/Tonsure: The shaving of a small part of the head. This was a Roman Catholic custom carried out as a man entered on the first steps of priesthood which persisted into the twentieth century.

Two Standards: One of the key contemplations in the second week of the 'Spiritual Exercises' (see above) in which a person prays to be received under the Standard of Christ.

Vatican II: The Second Vatican Council opened in 1962.

Vicar General: A priest appointed and delegated by a diocesan bishop to carry out certain legislative duties which are the bishop's responsibility.

Suggested Reading

Beginning

William J O'Malley SJ, *The Fifth Week* (Loyola University Press, 1976).

Ignatius St Lawrence SJ, *Ignatius Founder of Jesuits* (St Paul Publications, 1990).

Intrigued

Philip Caraman SJ, *Ignatius Loyola* (Collins, 1990).

Peter H. Kolvenbach SJ, interviewed by Renzo Giacomelli, *Men of God, Men for Others*.

William A. Barry SJ, *Finding God In All Things* (Ave Maria Press, 1991).

William V. Bangert SJ, *A History of the Society of Jesus* (Institute of Jesuit Sources: St Louis, 1972).

John O'Malley, *The First Jesuits* (Harvard UP, 1993).

Hooked

Ed., George E. Ganss SJ, *The Constitutions of the Society of Jesus* (Institute of Jesuit Sources: St Louis, 1970).

Ed., George E. Ganss SJ, *The Spiritual Exercises* (Institute of Jesuit Sources: St Louis, 1992).

Ed., William J. Young SJ, *Letters of St Ignatius of Loyola* (Loyola University Press, 1959).

Trans. by William S. Young SJ, *St Ignatius' Own Story* (Loyola University Press, Request Reprint, 1980).

Javier Osuna SJ, Trans. by Nicholas King SJ, *Friends in the Lord* (The Way Publications, 1974).

Thirty-Second General Congregation (The Way Supplement, Nos. 29/30, 1977).

Ignatian Horizons 1491–199 (The Way Supplement No. 70, 1991).

Simon Decloux SJ, Trans. by Cornelius M. Buckley SJ, *The Ignatian Way* (Loyola University Press, 1991).

* Denotes primary source material